Easter Is Coming

A Devotional Journey with Jesus

Christopher Greer

 ISBN-13: 978-0692373743 (M Street Publishing),
ISBN-10:0692373748

Italics in Scripture quotations are the emphasis of the author.

Preface

Before you begin reading, a short introduction about the kind of book this is and how to best use it will be helpful.

Easter Is Coming is organized around forty daily readings and seven days of reflection that cover, in chronological order, the events in Jesus' life that led to his crucifixion and resurrection.

Easter Is Coming is designed to begin on a Wednesday (like Ash Wednesday at the beginning of Lent), so each Day of Reflection falls on a Sunday. However, I encourage you to plan your reading so the Days of Reflection fall on whichever day of the week is the most restful for you.

Each day begins with a scripture passage. Start by carefully and prayerfully reading the day's Bible passage then read the devotional that accompanies it. The scripture passages are listed, but not quoted in full, to encourage you to find the passages in your own Bible and highlight or make notes around them. *To be familiar with God, we need to be familiar with scripture, and reading from your own Bible will help in that pursuit.*

Each day concludes with questions and instructions for reflection. Use this section thoughtfully and it will help you focus on what God says in that day's passage and how he wants to lead you and change you by it.

The words in this book were written to help illuminate and point to scripture. When they accomplish this task, use them. When they do not, set them aside and focus on what God teaches you in the passage alone. The Holy Spirit is the best guide!

Don't read alone. God has not designed you to be alone during this or any other time of year. Use *Easter Is Coming* as a guide for your friends, family, colleagues, Bible study group, or entire church. Gather regularly with others to talk about what God is teaching you and what each person is experiencing as you prepare to celebrate Christmas.

My prayer is that while reading scripture and *Easter Is Coming* you will be swept away by the beauty and power of Easter - the most important and life-changing event in history. I hope that over the next forty-seven days you will reflect on God's grace anew, allow it to continue to change your life, and share it with anyone and everyone you can.

Christopher Greer

Easter Is Coming

Introduction

Easter Is Coming is a devotional guide through Jesus' teachings and experiences on his way to the cross. It is designed to help you recognize and value the humility of Good Friday and the glory of Easter Sunday, and it can be read any time of year as a powerful reflection on Jesus' giving of his life in place of our own.

Regardless of the time of year, I encourage you to set aside the next forty-seven days with a Bible in one hand and this book in the other, and let God remind you again just how meaningful Easter is when you take the time to prayerfully make the journey with Jesus.

Day 1

Matthew 21:1-11

Ash Wednesday and Easter Sunday

"Praise God....Blessings on the one who comes in the name of the Lord! Praise God..."

In the spring of every year, much of Christendom begins the Lenten season by attending an Ash Wednesday service where their focus is trained on confession, repentance, and sorrow over sin. In these services (one of which I hope you plan to attend if you're reading this on Ash Wednesday), clergy and elders apply ashes in the shape of a cross to the foreheads of repentant congregants. There is deep solemnity on Ash Wednesday. There is the contriteness and humility that comes with the realization that we are sinful and in need of forgiveness that can only be given by the gracious Son of God.

Ash Wednesday's focus on our sin presents a dramatic contrast to Jesus' entry into Jerusalem. He was met on the road by an adoring public who worshiped him in word and action. They threw their cloaks and tree branches to cover the road in front of him while throwing their words of worship up to the God who sent him. It was a scene of great joy! A scene of excitement! It was the opposite of our quiet Ash Wednesday introspection.

Or was it? Perhaps worship and solemn reflection go together. After all, doesn't the worship of God lead us to humble repentance? Wouldn't the answer to their question "Who is he?" lead them to ask, "Then who am I?" How can we bear witness to his holiness without being confronted by our own depravity? How can we joyfully anticipate Easter Sunday's power without mournfully remembering our weakness?

Now it makes sense. Ash Wednesday inaugurates forty-seven days of fasting and confession to prepare for the greatest celebration of all.

There is another beautiful aspect about this moment in Jesus' journey: those who proclaim "Blessings on the one who comes in the name of the Lord!" (v. 9) unconsciously hit the nail on the head. This mysterious miracle-working man who rides in on a donkey has indeed come in the name of the Lord. It may not seem like it when he hangs from a tree on Good Friday, but it does when he walks out of the grave on Easter Sunday.

Through the next forty-seven days let us remember that Jesus is not God because he was resurrected – he was resurrected because he is God. He has been God forever. And he will be God forever. He was God when he created the world by the power of his spoken word, when he was born in a manger, when he chose his disciples, and when he healed the sick. And he was God the day he rode into Jerusalem.

In the upcoming weeks, my prayer is that you allow yourself to be just like the crowd the day he arrived in Jerusalem: they worshiped and they wondered (v. 9-10). My prayer is that you come to Jesus with a new sense of worship and wonder as you journey with him these coming days. Worship the king who has come, and repent as the sinner you are. It is a season for both.

Reflection

What is the most difficult thing you need to repent of?

What is the most wonderful thing about Jesus to you?

Spend the day prayerfully thinking about Jesus and your sin, and how they intersect – on Ash Wednesday and Easter weekend – and every day in between.

Day 2

Luke 19:41-44

A God Who Knows and a Man Who Weeps

Have you ever loved someone so much, or cherished a place so deeply, that the very idea of its harm would leave your cheeks stained by tears? I've seen this kind of love in my friend's eyes when his beloved church burned to the ground. I heard it in my brother's voice when his wife was undergoing cancer treatments. I've seen it in the face of a parent who helplessly watched their child make self-destructive decisions. These things are painful. And we weep.

One of the great mysteries - and necessities - of the incarnation is the full humanity and full divinity of Jesus. Here in Luke's account of Jesus' entrance to Jerusalem, we get a powerful glimpse of both. Jesus - who is fully divine - views the future as the present and knows it with perfect accuracy. He knows that his chosen people, despite their worshipful welcome just a few moments before, will reject him as King in a few days and will be destroyed by their enemies in a few decades. Jesus - who is also fully man - is overcome with emotion at the thought of both future realities. And just as he did at the death of his friend Lazarus,

Jesus wept (John 11:35). Jesus the divine, sees the outcome of Jerusalem's continued rejection of God, and Jesus the man, cannot withhold his tears.

This is the remarkable God you follow – or can follow today if you do not already. This is the remarkable Jesus who we honor with joyful celebrations each Sunday and with sacrificial surrender of ourselves each day. This Jesus is the one who knows that our self-serving actions, our self-satisfying religion, and our self-appointed god-ness manipulates and hurts others. He's the one that knows our rejection of God, our preference for sin, and our refusal to finally let go of ourselves will ultimately destroy us. And he weeps because of it.

Just like in Jerusalem 2000 years ago, Jesus knows the darkness of our hearts and he still rides into the center of it, dies the death only a man could die, and he gives the forgiveness and grace that only God can give.

As we march together towards Calvary and the empty tomb, keep in mind the Jesus we see in these four verses - fully man and fully God. He fully experienced what we all do, and fully accomplished what none of us can.

Reflection

Spend a few moments writing down what it means to you that Jesus was and is fully man and fully God. Thank him for the incarnation, even if you don't fully understand all of its mysteries.

Of the people you know and interact with, who do you feel sorrow over because he/she knows about Jesus the man, but rejects him as God? Remember their name all day today and pray they will turn to and follow Jesus.

Day 3

John 12:1-11

Don't Miss Jesus

I have gone to church for a really long time. Over the years I've gone for a variety of reasons; one being because it is my job. I've often approached church on Sunday as work, not as worship. But recently God reminded me again why I'm supposed to be going.

My wife and I were recently reading through the book of Ecclesiastes and when we reached verse 1 of chapter 5, Jesus shouted at me - seriously. It was one of those times when the words jumped off the page, rang in my ears, and provided a new, God-given intelligence pointing me in a different direction.

Ecclesiastes 5:1a reads "As you enter the house of God, keep your ears open and your mouth shut."

Instantly I knew God was asking me to reorient myself in regards to church. He was asking me – no, telling me - to go into his house ready to listen rather than talk. He wants me, you, all of us to focus on what we hear, not on what we say.

As a long-time church goer and church staff member, I often struggle with viewing worship in terms of what I offer to God and to others. In church, I have sung to God, prayed to God, given money to God. In church, I often encourage others, pray for others, talk to others, and teach others. I'm there so God and people can receive from me. In one sentence - "Keep your ears open and your mouth shut." - Jesus reminded me that this coming Sunday, and all those after it, is not about me. It's about him.

Jesus gives a similar reminder to Judas Iscariot in John 12. Judas is most famous for betraying Jesus, but here we see that before that fateful deed, he had long made the following of Jesus about somebody other than Jesus. At first glance we don't want to fault Judas for saying that Mary's perfume, used to worship Jesus, "should have been sold and the money given to the poor." (v. 5) It's a good idea. It's something a follower of Jesus would do. In fact, sometimes while reading this I'm invited to think *Jesus* is the selfish one! Doesn't he command us to give to the poor? Doesn't he teach us to be good stewards of our money? Then why let this woman pour a year's worth of money all over his feet? Doesn't Jesus know how many people that could feed?

Yes he does. But, Jesus also knows that Judas is not

following him because of Jesus. Judas is following him because of Judas. In the very next verse, scripture says Judas "was a thief" (v.6) that embezzled money given to benefit the poor so he could benefit himself. Jesus reminds Judas - and each of us - that our life with Jesus is about him and him alone. Life with him isn't about *only* his instructions (giving to the poor, going to church, etc.). It's also about worshiping Jesus. And out of a life of worship comes a life that does what he instructs. Like Judas, if we miss him when he is right in front of us, then we will always miss him.

It's only the third day of this devotion, but I need to ask a difficult question: Is your faith about Jesus, or about you? Is your Christianity about church? Tradition? Self-sacrifice? If your Christianity is primarily about anything other than knowing and being with Jesus, then not unlike Judas, your faith in Jesus is all about you.

Reflection

In your life, what instructions of Jesus have become about the instruction, and not about the instructor? Spend a good amount of time today thinking about why.

In all there is to do, learn, say, and accomplish today, don't miss Jesus. Write down one character trait that makes Jesus worth worshiping. And worship him for that trait all day today.

Day 4

Mark 11:12-26

Wait For It

This passage is awesome. It's also difficult. Why? Because there is a lot going on, because Jesus does a few things we don't expect, and because he says some things we don't understand. Each of these contributes to the passage's awesomeness and difficulty. I hope you will read it more than once today and see what stands out to you. Because there's so much here, allow me to share a few topics I've heard preached from this passage. Then I'll share what I found anew in it today. I'm sure one will provide you with food for thought.

My favorite sermon themes on this passage:

- Jesus is fierce. He cannot, and should not, be reduced to a teddy-bear – a soft, cuddly guy who above all else is nice, wants you to be nice, and teaches nice things. Jesus is God, and therefore he is powerful, hates evil, and is fiercely protective of what is his (including you). As C.S. Lewis said of Aslan in *The Lion, the Witch, and the Wardrobe* - "He is not safe. But he is good."

- Jesus loves God's presence and Jesus is God *in* the present. Therefore, he loves and protects the Temple.

- The church is not a place to conduct monetary business – it is a place to conduct spiritual business. Caution to those who reduce the latter to the former.

- Pray hard. God does not teach that prayer is a formula to get what you want, but he does teach that prayer is powerful and life-changing. And he wants us to do it.

Below is a theme that came anew to me as I read this passage. Reading John's account will help.

Read John 2:14-22 and pay close attention to verses 19-22.

Sometimes what Jesus says and the way he acts does not have clear and immediate meaning for us. Sometimes we have to wait for it. In Mark's account, Jesus confuses his disciples when he curses a fig tree. In John, Jesus frustrates the temple leaders when he claims they will destroy the Temple and he will raise it in three days. We, too, are a bit perplexed when these verses are read alone. Thankfully, Jesus is God, so he is the greatest teacher the world has ever known, and if his students have the patience to wait for it, they will learn the lesson the teacher intends.

The morning after Jesus curses the fig tree, his disciples learn that Jesus' words are powerful and have life-altering effects. Jesus uses their realization as an object lesson to remind them of his power and to teach them that through him their words of prayer can also have powerful, life-altering effects. In regards to the temple, it is not until his resurrection that the disciples - and some of the Jewish leadership - realize that the "temple" they destroyed was indeed "rebuilt" in three days. Jesus – the presence of God among them – is the new temple, and no grave can hold him.

Today as you pray, remember that God's timing is often different than ours.
Wait for it.

Today, as you continue through your day-to-day, remember that the benefits of sacrifice and discipline are not always immediately received.
Wait for it.

Today, as you look at scripture and the world around you and do not fully understand what God is up to, remember that he is the greatest teacher, and his lessons will be learned.
So wait for it.

Reflection

Why is it difficult to wait for the thing(s) God has told you?

What is something God has taught you that you now understand but did not at first?

Today, thank God for all he has taught you and commit to trusting him to continue to do so.

Day 5

Day of Reflection

For many of us, Sundays are the last day of the weekend before we jump headlong into another week of work, school, raising kids, and other duties and chores. Genesis tells us that God took a rest on the 7th day, and he even included keeping of the Sabbath as one of the Ten Commandments for the Jews. He's a fan of rest. Many of you are Christians, and most of you are Christians who fill Sundays with hard work for the church, and presumably Jesus, on this day of rest.

Decide today to make the next five Sundays (or whatever day you can commit to) days of rest and reflection. I’m not suggesting you call in sick for your duties as a Sunday school teacher or an usher, unless those duties get in the way of your ability to have at least one day devoted to rest. Instead, I’m encouraging you to set apart as much of this day as you can to restfully enjoy your God, your family, your freedom, and your life.

Don’t think about tomorrow. Do think about God.

Don't work. Do rest.

Don’t run. Do walk.

Don’t talk. Do listen.

“Be still and know that I am God.” - Psalm 46:10

Day 6

Matthew 21:23-32

The Gospel for Some

I have a friend, a follower of Christ, who won't share his faith with everyone any more. Before you judge him and wonder exactly what kind of follower of Christ this guy is, let me explain his situation and the wisdom behind it.

My friend works in an environment that is hostile to the Gospel. I don't just mean a place where he is outnumbered. He works in Hollywood for a company that regularly produces material that attacks the tenets of Christianity. The main creative force behind the content is an outspoken atheist who has been quoted as saying, “the world will be a better place when there are no more Christians.” Not exactly the kind of boss that approves of a Bible study in the break room.

But, with that said, my friend does not refrain from sharing the Gospel because he's afraid of his secular atheist colleagues. His restraint is not a matter of fear, but of efficacy. It's not a matter of who asks, but of why they ask. He uses the Lord’s discernment and wisdom in him, and the Holy Spirit's prompting to know the difference. He says, "I can easily tell when someone is using their questions to attack my faith, and when someone is asking questions to learn about my faith. I know when someone is asking my Christian view on homosexuality, abortion, or Jesus' claim to exclusivity simply trying to portray me as hateful and bigoted. Conversely, I also know when someone is asking me questions about God, prayer, and my decision to follow Christ because they genuinely want to know about Christianity. There is a distinct difference. And I will always answer the questions of the latter, but rarely entertain the former."

Clearly, my friend drew his wisdom from Jesus in the passage you just read. Take another look. Why does Jesus return their question in verse 23 with a question of his own in verse 24-25? If you look at the response of the elders and priests in verses 25-26, then you get a glimpse into their mindset, and gain clarity on Jesus' answer. He is not being elusive. He is discerning. He is not running from them. He's seeing if they will run *to* him.

Here we see these members of the religious elite as petty and ego-centric. They are so concerned with preserving their own hold on power that they are not interested in Jesus' true identity. They know John the Baptist was a prophet, and if they would have simply admitted this, I think Jesus very well could have revealed that he was the one John was prophesying about. But these men are not concerned with the truth. They want to paint Jesus as a heretic; something he's not. Sound familiar?

"To those who listen to my teaching, more understanding will be given, and they will have an abundance of knowledge. But for those who are not listening, even what little they understand will be taken away from them." - Matthew 13:12

There are few commands that are clearer than Jesus' command for us to share the Gospel (Matt 28:20). He makes it clear that we also will be rejected (John 15:18-21). And in today's passage it is clear that Jesus uses his God given wisdom to protect the truth from those who do not even know they are not ready to hear it. This is a tough line to walk. But my friend prayerfully encourages me by saying, "You'll know." Let me encourage you with the same.

Reflection

What is the most difficult thing for you about sharing your faith with non-believers?

What is the name of one person in your life – a family member, friend, co-worker, acquaintance – that is hostile to the Gospel?

Spend the next 5 minutes in prayer. For the first 2 minutes, ask God to give you courage and wisdom. For the last 3 minutes, pray specifically for the name you thought of (or ask God to give you a name) and ask God to soften their heart, and to sincerely desire the truth. Then pray for the courage to tell them that truth.

Day 7

Mark 12:1-12

Signed the Lease

This is a chilling parable, particularly for Jesus' primary audience, the first century Jewish religious leaders.

Many times in the Gospels, when parables are told by Jesus, the Gospel author does not tell us the response of the audience. Occasionally, when the audience is the disciples, the writers record their response to the parable and Jesus' explanation of it. Here in Mark 12, the writer of Mark tells us that the audience – the leading priests, teachers of religious law, and the elders - knew exactly what Jesus was saying. They knew they had been represented in the parable, and they knew the representation wasn't pretty.

Jesus, speaking as the son of the landowner, reveals that he is the landowner's final attempt to claim what is his – the lives of his people. He has entrusted these lives to the religious leaders, as he had done with the Jewish people since the day he chose them, and they have repeatedly disobeyed God, led the people astray, and tried to lay claim to what was not theirs. The

Jewish leaders, despite knowing this story was both biographical and a warning, remained resolved to hold the "estate" for themselves.

Dark. Violent. Threatening. It's not a cheery parable. But there is one part of God's promised justice that shines bright. Read verse 9 again. Did you see it? The very last part of the verse, "....and lease the vineyard to others."

This is the beauty of being a "New Testament" people! We know how this turns out! We know that Jesus wins and expands the list of chosen people! The only thing the religious leaders understood was that Jesus knew their hearts – better than they did – and, he used stories to reveal their inner thoughts to them and to others. But we know that the landowner's son defeats evil, and because of his love for all humanity, his resurrection from the dead opened the doors for the vineyard to be leased to "others."

Who are the others? You, me and anyone else that would follow; both the Jew and the Gentile. We are the blessed "others" God has leased his land to, allowing us the privilege to receive all that he has in return for all that we are.

What are you doing with the vineyard he has leased

you? What are you doing with your mind, body, health, money, work, relationships? What are you doing with your home, car, hobbies, time-off? What are you doing with your religion, your church, your relationship with Christ? Are you controlling all those things so that you can take over the estate? So you can keep all that has been leased to you for yourself? Or are you turning these things over to the rightful owner, working hand in hand with him to produce more and more blessing for more and more people?

Reflection

What is something God has leased to you that you need his help in returning to him?

Sit still for a few minutes, and prayerfully imagine that thing – that blessing - sitting loosely in the palms of your hands. Will you trust God when he adds more to your hands *and* when he takes something away?

In what ways is your relationship with Christ a blessing for you? In what ways is that relationship intended to be a blessing for others?

Day 8

Matthew 22:1-14

The Great Invitation

Just as we saw in yesterday's devotional, Jesus is serious about following him. Keep in mind that as Jesus tells this story, he stands in the temple, teaching all who will listen – in particular the religious leaders of the day. Jesus tells stories to reshape their understanding of the Kingdom of God. In their minds, the Kingdom of God was *their* kingdom. In their eyes, they alone held the keys to the temple; they alone could read and decipher the law; and they alone could determine if the miraculous was of God or not. So, Jesus stood in their midst and corrected their vision.

Have you ever felt like you were the one who always did the inviting, and if you didn't invite people to get together, no one ever would? Friendships can feel one-sided for the consistent invitation giver. Jesus reminds the Jewish leaders that they, the chosen race, have been invited repeatedly by the King. As we see throughout the Old Testament and now in the New Testament, they keep sending a "No thank you" as their RSVP.

So, God responds by changing things up a bit. This is my favorite part of this parable. In verse 9, the King takes a limited, VIP guest list, tears it up, tosses it to the wind, and his messengers yell out, "Come one, come all, to the greatest feast of them all!" This is one more aspect of what we celebrate at Easter. God, through the outstretched arms of Jesus, on the cross, says "Come one, come all!" His is no longer an invitation for the few. The time has come to invite everyone. Regardless of your nationality, your race, your past, or your sin – come one, come all. Good Friday is the Great Invitation, and Easter Sunday is the Great Celebration.

But there is a stern warning to those who have received the invitation. Verse 8 reminds us that in his love, God gives us the freedom of refusal. But his invitation has a shelf-life (Romans 1:21-26a). The honor of attending the party – even of being invited – is bestowed on us by the King, and is confirmed by our decision to follow. Without the latter, we lose the former. No acceptance, no invitation.

Through the cross, Jesus is inviting you to something that will bring more joy than you have ever experienced. Your joy may be to follow him for the first time. It may be to follow in more faith. It may be to give up a bit more of your selfishness by doing something you don't want to do for someone who needs you. It may be to give up obsessive self-improvement that only ends in self-chastisement. It may mean to drop church language for a relaxed conversation with your savior. It may be to walk to the foot of the cross, accept the all-encompassing love and freedom found in Christ, and breathe a sigh of relief as all the weight of your imperfection is lifted off your shoulders.

The cross is the Greatest Invitation. It's for everyone. It's for you. How do you need to respond?

Reflection

Is there an invitation that Christ has sent you? What is the invitation? How have you responded?

Why have you responded this way to his invitation? Spend a few moments prayerfully to reflect on his invitation and your response.

This parable makes it clear that the Kingdom of God has messengers, sent by God, to invite people to a feast for, and with his son. Are you one of those messengers that carry an invitation to others?

Day 9

Matthew 22:15-22

That's My Boy!

I don't know if fathers still do this anymore, but my dad refers to all of his sons, as “son.” Still today, at 34 years of age, my dad will say, “How are you, son?”, or “Have a good day, son”, or “I love you, son.” When we're all together (a rare occasion these days), and one of my brothers or I does something silly, Dad will lovingly and sarcastically quip, “that's my boy!” The beauty of the phrase is that he means it - in those silly moments and in the most special of moments. I can guarantee that when my dad listens to one of my younger brothers' newly recorded albums, or when he walks into a building designed by my older brother, or when he hears me preach on a Sunday morning, the phrase running through his mind while he smiles is, “that's my boy.”

Besides his declaration of it, my sonship is seen in other ways; most recently through my wife. After just a few years of getting to know my dad, she already has noticed and commented that I’m “just like him.” In some moments I bear his likeness. In most moments I bear his disposition and idiosyncrasies. In all, I bear his image.

In this passage in Matthew - also recorded in Mark 12 and Luke 20 - the religious leaders we have read about this week are now trying to trap Jesus. They live in a Roman occupied world where all devotion is due to Caesar. In one of Jesus' most famous responses to their weak attempts to paint him as an anarchist, he teaches them that there is the stuff of this world, and the stuff of heaven. And Jesus not so subtly implies that Caesar can have the stuff that bears his image, but God will have the stuff that bears his.

"So, God created human beings in his own image. In the image of God he created them; male and female he created them." - Genesis 1:27

As you walk through these days between Ash Wednesday, a day of repentance, and Good Friday, the day Jesus died for all of our sin, the tendency can be to focus on who we are not. And while understanding our sinfulness is important as we humbly approach God in repentance, we dare not forget what God thinks of us and the reason he made this earthly trip. He came because we are ***his***; because he loves us ***so very much***. Because you and I are his kids, his prize, his masterpieces, his greatest joy, and he will not stand for our separation. Out of his love he has made a way. Out of his love he has endured the cross. Out of his pride, joy, passion, and love he calls you his own.

You and I belong to God. And the proof is in the image we bear. He calls us son. He calls us daughter. In our silliest moments and in his most proud moments, he says, “That's my boy!” and “That's my girl!”

“Even before he made the world, God loved us and chose us in Christ to be holy and without fault in his eyes. God decided in advance to adopt us into his own family by bringing us to himself through Jesus Christ. This is what he wanted to do, and it gave him great pleasure.” - Ephesians 1:4-5

Reflection

The action of re-writing what we read is proven to help us remember it. So, write these verses down and put them in your pocket. Read them, and enjoy them, several times today.

“For we are God's masterpiece...” - Ephesians 2:10a

“He will rejoice over you with songs.” - Zephaniah 3:17b

“Your new name will be “The City of God's Delight” and “The Bride of God”, for the Lord delights in you and will claim you as his bride.” - Isaiah 62:4b

“For the Lord delights in his people.” - Psalm 149:4a

Day 10

Luke 20:27-40

Life After Death

Are you tired of these religious leaders yet? You could write a book on patience based solely on Jesus' interaction with the never-ending cynical questions of the Pharisees and Sadducees. Yet Jesus never stops engaging them, answering them, and strongly pointing them to the truth. Today we are the benefactors of their barrage of questions and Jesus' instructive answers.

Throughout the Gospels, Jesus has a powerful ability to see the heart of the questioner through the question. Look carefully at this passage again. The writer of this Gospel knows (and Jesus knows) the Sadducees believe there is no afterlife (v. 27). Again the religious elite try to make Jesus stumble over his words so they can label him a heretic and a fraud. They are willing to appear to compromise their own beliefs in order to do so. They frame a question about who will be married to whom in the hereafter. It is a strange question for a group that does not believe in an afterlife. Jesus acquiesces, and answers their question. But then he focuses everyone's attention on the question in their hearts, rather than the one in their mouths.

Their real question is not about marriage in the afterlife, but rather is there an afterlife at all? Jesus answers it in an intriguing way. He reminds them that Moses – their religious father whose teachings they used to try to stump Jesus – knew and taught the resurrection of the dead. Moses was told by God that He *is* the Lord (present tense) of Moses' deceased (past tense) forefathers (Exodus 3:6). Those who follow God on earth, live with him forever in heaven. There is a resurrection to eternal life for those who are found in Christ.

Do you see the point here? Jesus sets them up for belief in him – the first of the resurrected (Revelation 1:4-5). He uses the true beliefs of one of their religious forefathers to knock down their roadblocks to true belief. Jesus meets them on their intellectual level and prepares them for what they will never fully understand, but must fully believe to taste the blessing of resurrection for themselves.

And let's give credit where credit is due. In the final verses of this passage, the Sadducees cannot help but recognize that Jesus has met their intellectual demands. Is it belief in the one who will rise from the dead? Maybe not, but it's one step closer.

Reflection

What do you believe about the resurrection of the dead?

How do you see Jesus' teaching in this passage as pointing to the event on Easter Sunday?

Spend some time today to think about the hope and promise of resurrection from the dead for all who repent, believe, and follow the first who is risen, Jesus Christ.

Day 11

Matthew 22:34-46

If You Only Remember One Thing

How many times have you listened to a lecturer, a pastor, or even a friend, and heard them say this: "If you only remember one thing...." and it is then followed by the nugget of truth they deem to be the most important thing for you to know?

Do you sometimes read scripture and wish for the same thing? Don't you just want to close your eyes, flip to a random page, and have God show you the ***one*** thing, the only thing you need to remember from all he has written? Yeah, me, too.

Read Matthew 22:37-40 again.

Bingo.

This time the Pharisees question Jesus, with the intent to "trap him." Like the Sadducees before them, they don't seek the one nugget of truth that Jesus most wants them to know. They simply wait for him to slip up and say something they can hold against him. Again, unknowingly, their questions allow God to teach the nugget of truth he most wants *us* to know. So, here it is, ladies and gentlemen: it all boils down to this:

Love God. Love your neighbor.

Is that all? Don't I do that?

Love God. Love your neighbor.

I do feel love for God. And I do love people (Most people, most of the time. Or at least, some people some of the time).

Love God. Love your neighbor.

But what do I DO? What steps do I take? What skill do I acquire? What task can I perform? I need a rule, a law, a command, an instruction!

Love God. Love your neighbor.

I once heard a speaker say that he had stopped attempting to learn from scripture. He had recently read Matthew 22:37-40, and since Jesus himself said it was the greatest commandment of all the commandments, he was not going to try to do anything else Jesus said until he had mastered these two. He commented that everything else he had read seemed to fall under these two - just as Jesus said in verse 40. So, until he mastered them down, he wasn't worrying about the rest. I have no idea how it turned out, but I think it's a great idea.

So does Jesus.

We read scripture as though Jesus is simply the source of the instruction. But he's more than that. Jesus is the source of our very *ability* to obey his instruction. Love for him causes us to obey him, and obedience to him causes us to love others. Love God. Love your neighbor. Commandments? Yes, but also just facts.

For the Pharisees in the first century, and for us in the 21st century…"If you only remember one thing..."

Reflection

Love is an extremely important word in scripture. What do you think Jesus means here when he uses it?

Do an experiment today. Count the number of times you encounter the word "love" in a conversation, a song, a book, or on TV. Pay close attention to the objects of that love. Do we think our society ascribes more or less meaning to the word than Jesus? Think about your answer and its implications today.

Day 12

Day of Reflection

We would all likely agree that an important part of our gatherings on Sunday as Christians is worship through music. Worship of God has been happening since the Trinity created the very first angel. And with their voices they, and we, have told God who he is. And that is worship.

Today, pick three words that you attribute to God, from the list below or by writing your own, and use them to reflect on him and worship.

Powerful	Communicator	Forgiving
Creative	Loving	Giving
Listener	Generous	Kind
Redemptive	Perfect	Dynamic
Beautiful	Faithful	Absolute
Unique	Patient	Warm
Holy	Present	Steadfast
Hopeful	Graceful	Strong
Wise	Understanding	With Us

Day 13

Matthew 23:1-39

Repentance

Back on Day 3, we read a passage of scripture that opens a window to part of Jesus' character we don't often see or hear about; a side of Christ that, if we are honest, we don't often *want* to see or hear about. We see this part of Jesus again here in Matthew 23. Jesus is relentless when it comes to the hypocrisy of the teachers of the law and the Pharisees. I think this is true for two main reasons: 1) without repentance, there is no belief. We cannot follow Jesus and be in relationship with God if we ignore our own sin, and 2) these leaders were responsible for the faith of those they led. Jesus is very serious about our leadership, responsibility, and care for others.

With that in mind, I want to ask you to do something difficult today. I want you to read this passage again. This time, read it slowly and replace the words "teachers of religious law and Pharisees" with your name. Listen to the Holy Spirit through the words of Jesus as he shines light on our responsibility for our words and actions toward God and toward other people.

As uncomfortable or even painful as this may be, let the Son of God lay your sin bare, and allow him to lead you to repentance again today. As he does, repent. Confess and commit to follow him anew as he reveals all that keeps you from a pure relationship with him and with others.

Read the following verses and ask God to reveal to you what you need to repent of today. Respond as he leads you.

"*You do not desire a sacrifice, or I would offer one. You do not want a burnt offering. The sacrifice you desire is a broken spirit. You will not reject a broken and repentant heart, O God." - Psalm 51:16-17*

"*Zion will be restored by justice; those who repent will be revived by righteousness." - Isaiah 1:27*

"*If you warn them and they refuse to repent and keep on sinning, they will die in their sins. But you will have saved yourself because you obeyed me." - Ezekiel 3:19*

"*Repent of your sins and turn to God, for the Kingdom of Heaven is near." - Matthew 3:2*

"*I have come to call not those who think they are*

righteous, but those who know they are sinners and need to repent." - Luke 5:32

"In the same way there is joy in the presence of God's angels when even one sinner repents." - Luke 15:10

"Now repent of your sins and turn to God, so that your sins may be wiped away." - Acts 3:19

Reflection

How does reading this passage make you feel?

Is it difficult to imagine using this tone and language? Why or why not?

In what ways did you hear God tell you to repent? Write down one or more in your own words.

Day 14

Mark 12:41-44

Give Until It Doesn't Hurt

Have you heard the phrase, "give until it hurts?" Most of us have. Many of us have heard this phrase in church. The idea and intention behind it is good. The phrase plays on the idea of sacrifice, and it is used to remind us that it costs something to follow Jesus. It reminds us that to follow Jesus sacrificially is different than simply giving out of our excess, as Jesus points out in this passage. Following Jesus is about giving him everything.

The widow is a good, and an often referenced example. According to the words of Jesus, she has "given everything she had to live on." This is a big deal. Imagine giving everything *you* have to live on to God. I mean it. Imagine giving all of the $1500 or $15000 you make each month to God. All of it. Then think about this. If you literally gave all you had to Jesus, then who would you put your trust in? Yep. Exactly. Only Jesus.

Perhaps we should trade in the phrase "give until it hurts" for "giving is going to hurt." This would be

more honest, and would much more accurately reflect our feelings if we truly gave everything to Jesus. I hate to burst our health and wealth bubbles, but giving everything to Jesus is going to hurt. And it's going to hurt badly. We're all attached to our stuff –particularly our money, and all the things we think it affords us. Those who know this best are those who had everything ripped away from them. Their wealth. Their jobs. Their cars, homes, food, drugs, pleasure, and comfort. It hurts. It also hurts when in the course of following Jesus, we are called by him to voluntarily give everything to him. Our material possessions are one thing, our families, our health, and our safety are quite another. Handing these over to Jesus can really hurt. The people who have done it, or have *had* to do it know just how bad it hurts.
But here is the beauty of giving everything to God: once we have done it, we will never again have to give until it hurts. Once you give Jesus everything, then it is all his, and giving it away no longer hurts us.

The poor woman in today's passage did not give more money than the others. She never could. But she did give more spiritually than they had. But because she placed her life - her very livelihood - in the hands of God, giving her only "two small coins" was simply that: only two small coins.

The rich people aren't hurt by their giving because they haven't given it all. And the poor woman's giving doesn't hurt because she already has given her all.

Which do you think God can accomplish more with: the money of the rich, who have not yet given their lives, or the lives of the poor, who have no money to give?

Reflection

Some believers choose to prepare for Easter every year by giving up something for the forty-seven days of Lent. Some give up sweets or alcohol, while others sacrifice their time or talents. Have you given up anything for a specific period of time? If so, does it hurt because you have not already suffered the satisfying pain of giving everything to God? Or does it not hurt at all because you have already given all you have?

If you have given your all, what has God given you?

If you have not, what are you afraid of?

Spend a few moments to answer honestly and reflect on your answers today.

Day 15

Luke 21:5-19

Don't Miss the Trees for the Forest

This remarkable passage is probably richer to us, 2000 years after it was recalled and written, than it was to the original disciples who heard these words directly from Jesus' mouth. In all his glory, Jesus accurately comments on future events in his disciple's lives, the future of Jerusalem, and future events that have unfolded in the past 2000 years. Understandably, his disciples were filled with questions. "When will all this happen? What sign will show us that these things are about to take place? What sign will signal your return and the end of the world?"

As long as we have had scripture, we have asked the same questions. Type in the words "End Times" or "Book of Revelation" at Amazon and upwards of 10,000 titles will appear. Want to get fancy? Type in the fifty-cent word "eschatology" (a word in theology that means study of the end times) and you still get more than 5,000 hits. We are quite interested in the apocalypse, Jesus' return, the final battle, and the last days. The end has intrigued every people group from every corner of the planet since the beginning. But like the disciples, many times when we read this passage we miss the trees for the forest. And to give the disciples – and ourselves – some credit, Jesus talks a lot about the forest in this passage! But there is a very important tree we cannot miss.

Amidst Jesus' words about the destruction of the temple, kingdoms and war, earthquakes and famines, Jesus speaks about their individual lives. While he paints in broad strokes about the vast destiny of their city and world, he also attends to the tiny detail of their individual moments. In verse 12, Jesus uncovers a stark, violent, and insecure future for his followers. He tells them, "You will be dragged into synagogues and prisons, and you will stand trial before kings and governors because you are my followers." But unlike us and the disciples, Jesus never misses the trees for the forest.

Jesus reminds his disciples that in all of the bewilderment and chaos of their future persecution, God is most concerned with the individual souls of the creation he loves. These men and women will be wrongly accused, beaten, and eventually martyred. But Jesus says, "This will be your opportunity to tell them about me," and "I will give you the right words and such wisdom that none of your opponents will be able to reply or refute you!"

I don't know what you are experiencing during this forty-seven day journey. Maybe the whole world is falling apart around you, and like these disciples, you are looking for a sign - a way out - a signal telling you that all this chaos and destruction is actually the good work of God. But in the middle of the change and insecurity, don't forget about the people standing right in front of you - family members, co-workers, students, or strangers. Each is a creation of the God of the universe, and this may be your opportunity to tell them about his Son, Jesus.

Don't miss the trees. They won't survive in the forest unless other trees like you and me introduce them to the one on whom their very survival depends.

Reflection

Which trees are you likely to miss because of your concern for the forest?

Spend a few moments and ask God to develop your heart for the trees.

Day 16

Matthew 24:15-35

Reliable

As you read this passage you can understand why, as noted in yesterday's devotion, there are thousands of books about the end of days. It is fascinating stuff. Jesus, after speaking briefly of the trees in yesterday's passage, returns to the forest in today's passage. He gives us the truth of how everything will happen. And so far, he has been right on the money.

In Matthew 20, Jesus tells his disciples what will happen to him in Jerusalem, and after the fact, they recall their Lord's accurate prediction of his own death, burial, and resurrection.

Read it in Matthew 20:17-19.

In Luke's account of the speech you read in Matthew 24, Jesus tells his disciples that they will be persecuted and drug before courts because they follow him, and he promises the Holy Spirit will fill them with wisdom and the right words for the situation, and it happens. In Acts 4, after Jesus has gone to be with the Father, the exact circumstances take place. Peter and John are arrested because they preach about Jesus and they are dragged into court before the priests.

Take a few minutes to read Acts 4:1-21.

As you also read today in Matthew 24, Jesus outlines what will happen 40 years later when Rome destroys the temple and much of Jerusalem to end the Great Jewish Revolt. Like the events before, it happens just as Jesus said it would. In 70 A.D. Titus, the eventual 10th emperor of the Roman Empire, marches on Jerusalem with 70,000 men and destroys the temple and the city.

The good news found here is that Jesus is reliable; scripture is reliable. Just as he says in verse 35, "Heaven and Earth will disappear, but my words will never disappear." Here we are, two millennium later, reading through those very words. Indeed, they have not disappeared. Indeed, they are as meaningful and as full of saving grace as ever before.

One of my favorite passages in scripture is Revelation 21:1-5. The living Christ, in his revelation to John, tells again of the future, and it is as beautiful a picture as is painted in all of scripture. No more death. No more sorrow. No more tears. We will be with God, and he will be with us. I look forward to that day knowing that as Jesus' words have proven reliable before, they will prove reliable again.

Reflection

Turn to Revelation 21, and read verses 1-5.

If Jesus' predictions were accurate about his life, the lives of his disciples, and the life of the city of Jerusalem, then what hope does this Revelation promise bring?

Has God promised you something – by his word or his Spirit – he has reliably made good on?

When you recall it, spend the day in thankful worship for his reliability in your life, as well as in all of history.

Day 17

Matthew 24:36-51

Keeping Watch

As if the first few months of marriage aren't a big adjustment already, my wife and I decided to offer a bit of foster care for a family member's cat. Our family member could no longer care for the cat, so we took it until another, more suitable home was available. In our house, there were a few rules that differed from the last house where the cat had lived. Paramount among these was our "no bed" rule. This cat - as handsome, loving, and hypo-allergenic as he was - was not allowed on our bed. This took a bit of training. We would say "no" when he climbed up, and we would gently relocate him to the floor if he cuddled up at our feet in the middle of the night. And as the phrase doesn't really go, "when the humans are away, the cat will play" we frequently caught him on the bed after we had been away from the house for the majority of the day. In return we'd offer the appropriate scolding and it appeared he was learning. We began coming home to a cat happily perched on his blanket, away from the bed.

Then one day we left for a hike. After walking only a

few blocks from our house, we realized we had forgotten our water bottles and we flipped a U-turn and headed back to the house. We had been gone a scant 5, or 10 minutes, and as we stepped into our room, we caught our foster cat snuggling down for a nice long nap....on our bed! "The master will return unannounced and unexpected." There's no doubt that Gio, the cat, was taking after the evil servant and thought "My master won't be back for a while." Think again, Gio.

What does Jesus mean when he tells his servants to "keep watch" and "be ready all the time?" Does he mean for us to stand on the porch to keep a look out for the signs? Does he want us to study the before-mentioned thousands of end-time titles in hopes of discovering what the Mayans missed in 2012? Or is our role as faithful, sensible servants found in responsibly "managing his other household servants and feeding them (v. 45)?"

"You must love the Lord your God with all your heart, all your soul, and all your mind. This is the first and greatest commandment. A second is equally important: 'Love your neighbor as yourself.' The entire law and all the demands of the prophets are based on these two commandments."

Our keeping watch is our obedience. Our readiness is our trust and faithfulness with that which he has given us to do. He will return. Will we be ready? Will we be busy at the task of making much of Jesus? Will we be busy knowing, loving, serving, and giving to our neighbors? This is what it means to be ready, to keep watch, to live with expectancy for his return. And keep in mind, it may not be his early return that surprises us – it may be our early departure. Either way, we will face our loving creator, and our obedience makes us ready.

Reflection

We have been walking through forty-seven days of observance, preparation, repentance, and reflection. Has it also been a time of obedience and readiness through trust and faith? Why or why not?

As you continue to prepare for the celebration of his resurrection, do you also feel God ask you to prepare for his second coming? In what ways? (Just think and reflect on this today. Resist the urge to make a "to do" list.)

Day 18

Matthew 25:1-13

Only Children

One of the most insightful spiritual one-liners I've heard recently is "God has no grandchildren, only children." It's simple and cliché if you want to dismiss it. But, it's Biblically accurate and theologically profound if you think about it. First is the unspeakable and mind-blowing reality that we – mere mortals - by the saving blood, grace, and resurrection of Jesus become the sons and daughters of the living God. You've heard it a million times. But read it again, and let the unbelievable-ness of it strike you again. (If this is something you need to be reminded of - that because of Jesus you are an infinitely loved child of God - then spend this day remembering and celebrating it. Feel free to save the rest of this devotional for another day.)

The other, less obvious implication of this phrase is that your relationship with God must be exactly that: yours. Think of your grandfather and grandmother. You are only theirs because you are your parents' child. It doesn't work the same way with a relationship with God. You cannot be his simply because someone else is. He doesn't have any grandchildren, only children.

From time to time Jesus speaks of his final return by telling stories that help depict for his followers what it will be like. This story of 10 bride's maids is one of those stories, and the major theme is preparedness. But right in the middle, in verse 8, we learn again what it means to be a child of God. It is about us and our own personal preparedness to meet the groom. We cannot bum oil off anyone else. We cannot rely on the preparedness of others. We do not have an eternally secure relationship with our creator because one of our parents, grandparents, aunts, uncles, or siblings knows him personally. We may receive an introduction – like a blind date with the God of the universe - but once the introduction is made, we look him in the eye, we listen carefully to his invitation, and we trust and obey. Or we don't. An introduction is not a relationship. A grandchild is not a child.

There are few things that I am more thankful for than the beautifully personal relationships with Jesus that I observed in my parents. I am eternally grateful that my introduction to Jesus came from them at a very early age. As already stated, it's a blessing from God but not a relationship with God. It wasn't until college that I realized I had an impersonal relationship with church, not a personal relationship with God. And it could not be given to me or willed to me. It could only be taken up by me as I accepted the holy invitation of my Father and began to follow him, forsaking all else.

When it comes to knowing God, you can't borrow anyone else's oil. You can't read anyone else's Bible. You can't attend someone else's church. And you can't be the grandchild of someone else's God.

Reflection

Who do you know that believes they are a "grandchild" of God? Remember their name today, and pray in the power of the Spirit of God that they will meet him face to face, and walk with him hand in hand.

If you are that "grandchild," commit today to stepping out of the shadow of the one you know who believes, and find out what it means to believe and follow for yourself. You will never be sorry.

Day 19

Day of Reflection

Read Philippians 4:6-7.

Think briefly on one thing God has done in your life. Write it on a small card, post-it note, or in your phone, and thank him for it.

Now, think briefly of something God is doing now in your life. Record it with the other and thank God for it.

Last, think briefly about something God may do in your future and write down a word of gratefulness and offer it, or whatever may come, back to God.

Refer to these notes at each meal today and walk through the hours grateful for all God has done, is doing, and will do.

Day 20

Matthew 25:14-30

Buried Alive

I have a friend who works in a building with 25 or 30 people. Recently she has been treated unfairly, and while never one to complain, she is almost certain the treatment is because of her faith. Some of you know what this is like. None of us are spit upon, beaten, or burned at the stake, but we endure side glances, rolling eyes, disrespectful scoffs, untrue rumors, and name calling. Sometimes we wonder if we just kept our head down and our mouth shut, then maybe our work days would go uninterrupted.

For my friend, it is too late. Everyone knows why she doesn't work on Sundays, why she doesn't drink in excess, and why she defends those that are being gossiped about. We pray that someday soon they will realize the reason is the same reason she treats them respectfully, joyfully serves her clients no matter their mood, and is honest and fair in all her business dealings.

There are a couple other Christians among her colleagues, but unlike my friend, they keep their heads down and their mouths shut. And they are treated differently. No dirty looks and no disrespectful words. But if asked, few of their colleagues know they, too, are followers of Jesus.

This parable, often called the Parable of the Talents, is a familiar one. Unfortunately, in many of the scripture's stories, I miss what God wants to teach me because I already "know" the story. But today I am drawn in a new way to the last servant, the one who buries his master's money. Out of fear of losing it, or investing it poorly, or of having nothing to show for how he used that which he was given, the servant does nothing. He relegates the money meant for investing to currency kept for protecting. Like my friend's colleagues, this servant keeps his head down and his mouth shut. Instead of taking what his master has so generously given and allowing it the freedom to grow, no matter the risk, he buries it out of fear.

I'm guilty of doing the same thing. Unlike my bold and faithful friend, I often take the grace, forgiveness, and hope I'm given by my Lord, and I bury it in my fear, insecurity, and pride. Instead of opening it to the air and people around me, and allowing it to grow, I cover it up, fearful that others will shoot it down. In so doing, I self-proclaim that I am a "wicked and lazy servant."

But in response, God proclaims there is nothing to fear. *He* is the one who grows his investment. He is the one who multiplies his gift. He is the one that doubles his goodness. We are simply asked to fearlessly invest it in the lives of others.

"*The Lord is for me, so I will have no fear. What can mere people do to me?" - Psalm 118:6*

"*If God is for us, who can ever be against us?" - Romans 8:31b*

On Ash Wednesday, did you wipe the ashes off your forehead as soon as you left the church? Do you tell your friends why you do what you do? Do you invite them to your Easter service? Or have you taken what God has given you and buried it?

Reflection

Read Psalm 118:6 again. What thoughts and emotions does it well up inside you? Write them down.

Today, memorize Psalm 118:6. It's short. It's powerful. It's important. It's true.

Once memorized, recite it 50 times today, and allow the truth of it to penetrate your heart, not just rattle in your head.

Day 21

Matthew 25:31-46

Invisible People

You really should read this passage more than once. In fact, you should find a place where you can sit and absorb this powerful passage of God's word. Read it slowly and carefully. Stop to chew on the significance of each statement. Granted, we should do this with all of God's word, but this is one such passage in particular.

In verse 31, don't miss that Jesus is coming back in all his glory. In the next verse, don't miss the universal power of our Lord and Savior; EVERY nation will gather in his presence. Think about that for a minute.

In verse 32 and 33, when he refers to the sheep, don't forget that Jesus said, "I am the good shepherd." He knows his sheep and they know him, and he loves them so much that he sacrificed his own life for theirs.

Then, when you spend a few moments and marvel at the enormity of God's presence, glory, and sacrifice, notice that this unfathomable God is served and cared for when we serve and care for our fellow man. He doesn't require some sort of unknowable or impossible task. He asks for compassion. He doesn't ask us to find him in visions and dreams. He asks for us to love those we see around us. He doesn't stay on a throne in the sky to watch you attempt to reach to his level. He has come to our level, and he asks that we stay here and change the lives of the others on our playing field.

Do you struggle with invisible people? I do. I couldn't tell you the eye color of the coworkers I see almost daily. I don't know the names of most the people in my seminary classes. I couldn't tell you whether my barista this morning was a man or woman, was black or white, was happy or sad, or was poor in spirit or full of joy. He/she was invisible to me.

While facts like these, and this passage in general, are often used to make us feel guilty for not doing more to help the people around us in the name of Jesus, I want to point out the joyful simplicity of it.

This passage reminds us that serving Jesus and experiencing the face of God is as simple as noticing those that are typically invisible to us, and interacting with them: in particular the poor, marginalized, sick, and imprisoned. This task should give us joy and hope! It is simple to find people in these situations, so it is simple to find ways to serve Christ! Even if "simple" does not mean "easy," we should rejoice at God's clear direction, open our eyes, and serve and care for him by serving and caring for people.

Reflection

Close your eyes and take a mental journey through your typical day. Try to recall and name the people you interact with on a daily or weekly basis. Neighbors, co-workers, barista, grocery checker, receptionist, homeless person, lady walking her dog. If you can recall their names, can you recall one attribute about them? For those you can recall nothing about, make a point to notice them today.

What is a people group that is invisible to you? The homeless? Incarcerated? Elderly? Children? Poor? Jobless? Lost? Ask God to tell you today one way to become aware of this group of people.

Day 22

John 12:20-50

Shaliah

Shaliah is a Hebrew legal term that means "the one who is sent is like the one who sent him." It is like the term ambassador. An ambassador carries the authority, rights, and power of the one who sent him/her. Today we are most commonly aware of this in regards to government. The United States has ambassadors to virtually every nation on the planet, and those individuals represent the interests and legal authority of the United States government. It's a powerful position. It's a powerful concept.

To me, Jesus as "Shaliah" is one of the most intriguing and joy-inducing aspects of his incarnation. At Christmas time we celebrate his entrance into our reality as a baby - the same way we enter it. We marvel at the idea of God as a human. But as I read John's Gospel, the tables are turned, and I find myself marveling at the human as God.

What strikes me as I read the end of this passage is the pure beauty found in Jesus' words in verse 45, "*For when you see me, you are seeing the one who sent me.*" Shaliah. When we see Jesus, we see God. Let me repeat that. When we see Jesus, *we see God*!

Doesn't that just blow your mind? You - yes you - the one reading these words right now. You *know* what the most powerful, creative, holy, captivating, and valuable being in all of time and space is really like. You've seen him! I don't mean the cloak and beard or the sandals and smile pictured in a movie or musical about Jesus. I mean the attributes, the character and the person of God. Creator God, visible, understandable, relatable, hearable, knowable in the person of Jesus the Christ.

And the knowledge gets better. The knowing of Jesus Christ brings light to your darkness and eternal life to your death. *"I have come as a light to shine in the dark world, so that all who put their trust in me will no longer remain in the dark....The Father who sent me has commanded me what to say and how to say it. And I know his commands lead to eternal life."*(v. 46, 49)

Shaliah. I'll never fully wrap my mind around it, but I'll never stop trying. Jesus is God. God is Jesus. You know Jesus. You know God. Amen.

Reflection

List a few things you know about God because you have experienced them in Jesus.

Is “knowing God” a cliché or “old hat” to you? Why? What is it about knowing the God of the universe that could ever become boring or yesterday’s news?

If this is the boat you’re in, spend a few minutes today thinking of the grandeur of a God who created all you have seen and haven’t seen - even your ability to see anything at all. Then worship in wonder again.

Day 23

Mark 14:12-26

Delayed Understanding

Have you ever received a message from Jesus through scripture, prayer, a sermon, or another believer, that you did not understand until later? I have. One time in particular, the message was a very, very difficult one to understand and obey, and the purpose and meaning for it was not clear until much later. At first, I would have traded it for any other message. But after experiencing its meaning and purpose, I was thankful for the blessing and purpose God had in his message.

Think of today's passage again. Imagine being a disciple during these moments. Imagine you are a constant follower and close friend of this man who has forever changed your life and the world. He often spoke in parables and performed miracles that a regular person like you did not always understand, but each word and every action rang with truth. He made your life and the lives of others better, more whole, and more satisfied. On this night he spoke again of things you did not fully understand, but this time they did not resound with hope and healing. Instead he spoke of a traitor's work, sacrifice by death, and his broken body and spilled blood. This was not the kind of talk that should commemorate Passover. Or was it?

It was difficult for the disciples to hear Jesus predict betrayal among this group of close friends. Scripture tells us the disciples were “greatly distressed” when they heard Jesus' words. We can imagine the feeling. It must have been even more distressing to hear the Son of Man say, “The Son of Man must die.” Was he suicidal? Or did he really know much, much more than they thought possible? It would have been painful to be in that room that night. It would have been scary.

Truth be told, I don’t know why God sometimes reveals information in the way he does. I don't always get why he tell us to do things we don’t understand, go places we aren’t familiar with, care for people we are afraid of. I could give you all the positive “pastor” answers. But in the end, I do not truly know.

What I do know, from the witness of scripture and my own life, is this; it all works out. I believe that all told, it is undeniable in scripture that God cares for us *and* that he is in control. I also know it’s undeniable that it does not always feel that way. But the difference between us being in control and God being in control is often just a matter of feelings. Feelings fade. And just as we will read in a later devotion, the upper room confusion made all the sense in the world once the disciples gathered around the risen Christ. Our trust that God is in control means the same for us. We may not understand what he says now, but we can trust that later we will be thankful for what he does.

Reflection

Take a few moments to remember back to a time when you did not understand a message God was giving you. In the clarity of hindsight, what have you learned, and how that may be a good lesson even if it didn't feel good?

Some of you may be right in the middle of a difficult season similar to the disciples' upper room confusion. You may have no idea what, why, or if God is doing something good in your life. And it is probably very painful. Take a moment now to willfully trust God. Trusting God is not only a feeling. Particularly in times like these. Trust him. Allow yourself to. Will yourself to. And feel deeply the relief – even if it's only a little at first – your trust affords you.

Day 24

John 13:1-17

Foot Washer

Foot washing is an ancient custom that is somewhat lost on us today. I don't know about you, but I've never entered a neighbor's house and found a basin of water in which to wash my feet. The closest is when I go to my aunt's house and I take my shoes off at the door to protect her carpets from my dirty soles. But for an ancient traveler who wore sandals on his daily commute down dirt streets, washing his own feet upon entering another's home was customary, except for the rarest of occasions. At the very wealthiest of homes, the owner would send a slave to wash your feet for you. But to have anyone do this most humble of jobs was rare, and it was an act of humble service that few engaged in.

Genesis mentions foot washing in several verses. Then in 1 Samuel 25:41, Abigail responds to David's wedding proposal by saying, "*I would be happy to marry David. I would even be willing to become a slave, washing the feet of his servants!*" Abigail is using hyperbole. Washing feet is obviously nothing the bride of a king would do. She says it as a way of showing how unbelievably privileged she feels just to be invited into the house of David. For that privilege she would even be willing to take the very lowest of positions – a foot washing slave. And that is my point. Washing the feet of others is not something that is done by the master of the house, or any person of authority, privilege, or power. It is done by household slaves if done at all.

For this reason, foot washing is the perfect act to clearly demonstrate the character of God.

Look at the verse preceding Jesus' washing of the disciples' feet - verse 3. *"Jesus knew that the father had given him authority over everything and that he had come from God and would return to God.*" And what's the very next word? "*So.*" So he washed his disciples' feet.

If you're thinking, "What?? Wait, this doesn't make any sense!", then you're right. It does not makes sense for Jesus, the one given all the authority of God (as we saw in "Shaliah" two days ago), to bend down, hike up his clothes, and take on the job of a slave. Yet he does it. And here we see in full view what it means to be God - what it means to have "authority over everything" and to "come from God." It means to put yourself at the service of others.

He is the God of the Universe, ***so*** he washes feet. Not he's the God of the universe so he would never wash feet. It's like the crying, helpless baby at Christmas. It's like the wounded Messiah we discover dying on Good Friday. It is unexpected humility by the most powerful being in all of time and space.

This is the miracle of Christianity. God has come to us, to love and serve us, to show us how to love and serve others, and to call us to do it. He's not a faraway god who has not experienced this life or who asks us to do what he has never done and will never do. Instead he did what he never should have done to show us how to do what we proudly believe we should never do, knowing that as we follow the lead of this unexpected God we'll find unexpected joy.

Reflection

How have you discovered God to be different than your expectations recently?

Does it change your view of God? Why or why not?

Does it change your view of your role as a follower of this God? How?

Day 25

1 Corinthians 11:23-26

Symbols

I love Christmas. More accurately, I love all the stuff that seems to make Christmas, Christmas. The list goes in this order. Christmas lights. Christmas music. Christmas tree. Gift wrapping. Christmas desserts. When I see the first Christmas lights hung on someone's house, and when I hear the first playing of "Silent Night" or "Let it Snow," I am instantly filled with cheer. Literally. These symbols and practices immediately carry me into the joy of the season, longing for family, and the celebration of the Christ Child. One light. One note. One red and green box. That's all it takes.

Jesus knows the power of a symbol. I have no doubt that Jesus orchestrated his death during the Roman rule of Palestine in part because the cross would become the most lasting symbol of the saving work he accomplished on it. The cross is a powerful symbol.

Jesus does the same the night of his arrest. As Paul records in 1 Corinthians, after hearing directly from the mouth of the risen Christ, Jesus takes the Passover meal - a meal already full of symbolism - and gives it new meaning. You are likely familiar with it; a pinch from a loaf, or a diced up pita, or a thin wafer. A thimble's amount of juice, bread dipped in the cup, or a shared chalice of wine. It's called Communion, The Lord's Supper, The Eucharist. The bread represents his body, the wine represents his blood, and when we eat and drink of it, we commemorate what Jesus did on that cross.

We know these symbols. But do we *feel* these symbols? Like lights and Christmas music for me, are the bread and wine powerful symbolic reminders that flood you with the meaning of Jesus' sacrifice? Does the bread remind you of his body and his living a human life like you cannot live and dying a human's death like you deserve? Does the wine remind you of his blood, dropped with sweat at his greatest point of obedience, spilled during torture and death, and covering your sin?

This is why Jesus said, "Do this to remember me." We need symbols. We need reminders. And Jesus has given us these so we never forget what he has done for us. The next time you take and eat the bread, crushing it between your teeth, let it lead you into thankfulness that because of Christ you will never be crushed for your sin. When you taste the wine, let it remind you that because of Christ's victory over your sin you can now taste and see that the Lord is good.

Reflection

What does communion mean to you? Reflect on the symbols of the bread and wine and what they mean.

What is a symbol or action that helps you connect to Jesus in your life? I challenge you to pick one and carry it or practice it through Easter, and beyond. Here are some ideas.

- Carry a small cross in your pocket

- Buy a loaf of bread and wine or juice and take a taste of each at dinner each night.

- Light a candle daily to remind you of the Holy Spirit's presence with you.

- Carry your Bible - in your bag, your briefcase, or your car - as a reminder that the word was made flesh.

- Look for churches on your commute or when you drive, and allow them to serve as reminders that God came, and is calling a people to himself.

- Pick or buy a flower every day to remind yourself that God is the beautiful creator.

Day 26

Day of Reflection

God loves you. You've heard this before. In fact, you've probably heard it a ***lot***. (I hope!) But did you also know that God *likes* you? Did you know that he enjoys you?

Today, as you take a Sabbath rest – setting the day aside to simply be with God – enjoy the fact that God likes you. He wants to be around you. He does not do what he does for you reluctantly or out of obligation, but out of joy and enthusiasm and delight. His love is simple, innocent, and a beautiful delight.

Allow these words from God to remind you of his gladness in you today!

"*For the Lord delights in his people...*" - *Psalm 149:4*

"*He will take delight in you with gladness....He will rejoice over you with joyful songs.*" - *Zephaniah 3:17*

"*God decided in advance to adopt us into his own*

family by bringing us to himself through Jesus Christ. This is what he wanted to do, and it gave him great pleasure." - Ephesians 1:5

Day 27

John 13:18-38

Real

I have read and heard this story so much that its reality is easily lost on me. In my familiarity, Judas becomes a token bad guy; a bland piece of the Easter puzzle. And I'm not alone. In our day and time, Judas is just a cliché. His name is mentioned in movies, books, magazines, and even evening news stories that have anything to do with a traitor. "Judas" is only a word - a synonym of "betrayal" - not a real person in real time who did real things.

But Jesus' painful declaration that a deceiver was a member of his inner circle helps lead me back to the reality of Judas' choice. In verse 21, scripture says that Jesus was "troubled in his spirit" or "deeply troubled" with the knowledge that he would be betrayed. This wasn't just a throw-away scene in some story we've read a thousand times. These were real men, who shared deep friendship and love. The betrayer fell to the real enemy, and he made choices that sparked his friend's final turn to Calvary. The betrayed endured a real broken heart as he watched his close companion succumb to evil and give him the kiss of death.

This reality is the beauty of God's incarnation: Jesus as fully man and fully divine. Jesus was a ***real*** man. He hungered and thirsted, he felt pain and he wept. He bled and he died. And just like you and me, he was deeply hurt when his friends sold him out.

Jesus was also ***really*** God. Only God can face down evil, conquer death once and for all, and give the benefits of eternal life to greedy betrayers and selfish deniers.

Jesus, in his humanity, is crushed when a follower and friend is unfaithful or turns from him forever. Yet Jesus, in his divinity, conquered the consequences of sin, and leaves his open arms for all who confess and repent. Betrayers and deniers are still frequently found among Jesus' closest friends. And forgiveness and salvation are still just a confession away.

As one who is both betrayer and denier, I'm thankful for being forgiven and saved.

Reflection

Which scenes from scripture or in the life of Jesus have been most impacting for you? In contrast, which seem to have lost their real-ness? Why do you think that is?

Do you relate to Judas or Peter at all in this passage? If so, how?

Are you thankful for, or in need of, God's forgiveness? Confess your sin and prayerfully thank God for his grace.

Day 28

Luke 22:24-38

Headline: Jesus Christ fired as CEO

Jesus would never have been a CEO today.

Transpose this scene in scripture into a modern business setting. Jesus is the owner, creator, and CEO of a Fortune 500 company. In the boardroom - complete with a long polished table, comfortable swivel chairs, and glass windows looking out over the city from 25 stories up - Jesus has called a meeting with his board of directors. Here sit the most important men in the company awaiting important words from the head-honcho.

They admire their leader and know he is not like any other CEO in the world. He knows more and can do more than anyone else they've ever seen or followed. As they wait, they wonder aloud what this meeting is for. They are primed for winning words of wisdom, above average advice for attacking the competition, and insightful instructions for enabling their rise to the top. Their enthusiastic thoughts turn into hyperbolic talk about position, power, hierarchy, and control. He's dropped hints about retirement, but none of them can imagine it actually happening. And if it did happen - If Jesus were to leave - who will be his successor? Who is currently the most important and powerful? The questions quickly become comparisons of credentials and exaggerated resumes.

The jockeying becomes so fevered they barely notice that Jesus, their CEO, has entered the room. Finally, all eyes turn to him. The first words from his mouth gain their attention: "Among you it must be different." His second round of words bewilder them: "Those who are the greatest among you should take the lowest rank."

A new frenzied argument erupts as they quickly backpedal. Those who were just clamoring for the top rung now pretend to want a job in the mail room!

This was not the meeting they imagined. Jesus has turned the company on its head. He's announced the scandalous departure of one board member, and he's predicted the temporary resignation of another. And now, most shocking of all, he is claiming that the leaders sitting at this table must be servants of all their employees, clients, and potential clients.

These conversations captured in Luke 22 are inapplicable to us in the 21st century. In our day and age, leaders are not servants and servants are not leaders. That may have worked in the first century when Christianity was just a start-up, but now that it's a full-blown world leading company battling it out with Secular Atheism Inc., Islam.com, and a potential Buddhist/Hindu merger (not to mention the Mormon Org. and Spirituality LLC), servants don't win any battles. Jesus' approach is outdated and should be relegated to the docile family life and the lower classes who are not interested in getting ahead.

True or false?

Reflection

How does Jesus' teaching in Luke 22:24-27 contradict the world you operate in daily?

What gives Jesus the authority to teach that "among [us] it must be different" while still making the promises in verses 28-29? Is this a contradiction? Why or why not?

Look around you today and ask, "Who can I serve?"

Day 29

Matthew 26:31-35

A Sweet Meeting

Pride is a funny thing. Sometimes it pops up unannounced. Particularly, when our idiosyncrasies or our failures are pointed out by someone close to us. For instance:

- The phrase "You're just like your father" when the person saying it is referring to one of your dad's traits you were hoping to avoid picking up.
- When your husband or wife says "I don't like it when you..."
- When someone outside your family pokes fun at someone inside your family, even if the poke is warranted.
- When someone says, "I know you're going to fail again. You just can't help it."

In moments like these we summon all our strength and swear that we will never again act like our father, annoy our spouse, or fall into our destructive habit. We do the same thing with sin. We fail once, or habitually, and we promise ourselves and God that we will not dishonor him, ourselves, or others in this way ever again.

How does that usually turn out? Uh huh. I'm the same way.

And Peter too. Peter goes through this exact thing. Jesus tells all his disciples that they will desert him, and either Peter is less self-aware than the others or his rebuttal is recorded because he talks the loudest. Either way, he adamantly denies that he will abandon his Lord. Hearing Jesus' response, Peter's pride is injured even further. Jesus speaks truly when he says Peter will take it one step further than the other deserters: three times Peter will individually deny any association with Jesus.

I have always related to Peter. I am always saddened by his story because I see myself in it. But today, as I read this passage, I find in it a beautiful word of comfort from our Savior. It is tucked away neatly in verse 32. Jesus promises to meet them, after his resurrection, in Galilee.

It is such a sweet and powerful promise. Later we will focus on the power of "after I have been raised from the dead," but for now it's the words, "I will...meet you there," that I want to draw our attention to. Jesus just told his disciples that they would all leave him.

And they do. But he promises he will still meet them afterward. And he does.

No matter how many times we desert him and deny him, he will always meet us. This is the sweet promise I find comfort in while reading this passage. Jesus knows I will fail him. I know that Jesus knows I will fail him. But, I also know that he will still meet me. And that promise allows me to live in freedom and joy in spite of my future failures, instead of in guilt under the shadow of them.

Reflection

Read verse 32, and think on this sweet promise all day today. Regardless of your departure, he will meet you on the other side.

Day 30

John 14:1-31

I Am the Hamburger

John 14:6 is one of the most familiar and important verses to understand who Jesus is and what he does for us. It is also one of the most familiar. Some of you may know it by heart. Still I encourage you to read it again, and try to discover again (or for the first time) what is unique about it. Then read it slowly one last time realizing what it says about Jesus.

Jesus speaks these important words in response to a beautifully honest question by one disciple. You have to love Thomas' candor here. And Jesus' set-up is perfect. Jesus is talking about going to his rightful place at the right hand of the Father, and it's almost as though he forgets that his disciples still are not fully clear on what's about to happen. He seems to take for granted that they are on the same page with him. Thomas is the only one with enough guts to raise his hand in the back of class and say, "Hold on, wait a minute. We have ***no*** idea what you are talking about! How can we know the way??" (my paraphrase)

Jesus gives his critically important answer: "I am the

way."

Do you notice something strange about this answer? Maybe something that appears to be a grammatical error of some sort? People can't *be* the way. People cannot be any way! People can know the way, be on the way, and teach the way. But they can't *be* the way. Right?

Look at it again. When Thomas asks where he is going, Jesus doesn't say "I know the way, I know the truth, and I know how to have life." Instead, he says "I AM." *"I AM the way, I AM the truth, I AM the life."*

I think if I were Thomas I would have thought Jesus was crazy. I mean just imagine if someone said this to you today. Imagine you are on a road trip with your family, and while getting gas, you turn to the attendant and say, "My family and I are getting a bit hungry. Do you know where we can get a hamburger?" Wouldn't it be weird if he looked you in the eyes, held out his hands, and said, "I *am* the hamburger?" Weird? Flat out crazy. You wouldn't give that guy the time of day! You would jump in the car and tell your family to keep their eyes open for a Taco Bell.

But that is *exactly* what Jesus does. And that is what makes this such an important identity statement. All we need in life is Jesus. Period. Many men know many things. Some even know the way, the truth, and how to have life. But only one man can claim to ***be*** the way, the truth, and the life. And that man is either a lunatic, or he's God. Only God can be the end point of all our searching, all our questions, and all our needs.

Reflection

Is Jesus your absolute source - your way, your truth, and your life? Why or why not?

In what ways are you tempted to think of Jesus as simply *knowing* the way, the truth, and how to have life, instead of *being* the way, the truth, and the life? What's the difference to you, and why does it matter?

Spend today pondering the impossibility of this statement if it was made by a mere man. Contrast that with the important reality of this statement being made by God.

Day 31

In the introduction to this devotional guide, I encouraged you to focus on the scriptures, allowing each day's devotional to serve as an accompaniment to what God is saying to you through the Bible passage. I am reminding you of that goal now because the scriptures you will read during the next few days are so very powerful. Read them. Enjoy them. Ask for God to shape you by them and pay close attention to what he brings to the surface.

John 15:1-27, 16:1-4

Where the Water Flows

There is a beautiful phenomenon in Southern California. The trees grow where the water flows. That may seem like a total no-brainer, but this is rarely as visible as when in a desert climate like Southern California.

My bride and I went for a long hike in a nearby National Forest one Christmas Eve (I remind you again that we live in Southern California!). It was not long after exiting the I-15 freeway and passing a few strip malls before we found ourselves winding through sprawling ranches with large homes and horses with room to run. Once the terrain got too rugged for homes and grazing animals, we were surrounded by a range of desert mountains covered in scrub brush.

This particular hiking trail started by descending into a large ravine between two mountains, and the further we went down, the bigger the trees got. The day was perfect. The clouds hung low and the overcast sky made every color pop. The rain brought green to the grass, and the late cold snap brought yellow to the leaves. The trees big enough to have fall leaves were beautiful. But they were rare. They grew in very specific places; near the water.

You never had to wonder where the water flowed. You just had to look for the big, healthy, strong trees. All those away from the water were...well...small and unimpressive. The tree-lined creek-beds brought to mind Psalm 1...

Oh the joys of those who do not follow the advice of the wicked, or stand around with sinners, or join in with mockers. But they delight in the law of the Lord, meditating on it day and night. They are like trees planted along the riverbank, bearing fruit each season. Their leaves never wither, and they prosper in all they do. – Psalm 1:1-3

And this Psalm reminds me of verse 5, in today's reading from John:

Yes I am the vine; you are the branches. Those who remain in me, and I in them, will produce much fruit. For apart from me you can do nothing. - John 15:5

All you have to do to tell where God's word is read and obeyed is to look at the people. We are so similar to the trees. It's often easy to see which of us is passionate about God's word, and in love with the author. Those are the people that are growing. Those are the people that among all the trees that litter the hills, they are tall, strong, and vibrant. The key to their growth is living water.

No one in California goes to the mountains to see the small, scrubby, shrubs and trees. When they are in the mountains they want to see giant Redwoods, massive Oaks, and Eucalyptus trees that touch the sky. The same is true in our lives. When we plant ourselves near the “riverbank” and “remain” in him, we grow, and those watching will see where the water flows and will long to plant themselves next to it, too.

Reflection

How close to the living water are you planted?

Recall a time when you were planted far from the living water and did not remain in him. What was it like? How did it compare to times when you were absorbing the living water?

Day 32

John 16:5-33

Stuck in the Present

It's so refreshing how absolutely human Jesus' disciples were. Like many of us, they had their not-so-bright moments coupled with instances of wisdom. We get to see them afraid and self-centered as well as courageously serving others. In the first few verses of today's passage, I see in them what I see frequently in myself: fear of the unknown and an intense focus on the present. I don't blame them because I'm just like them.

The present – the here and now – is very difficult to let go of. Here, Jesus told his disciples that things were about to change, and he laid it on thick. He soon realized they were in denial and that they didn't want to accept the future ahead of them. Jesus recognized they are firmly stuck in the present.

In verse 5, Jesus said again, "I am going away." Then he made an interesting point. "And not one of you asks me where I'm going. Instead, you grieve because of what I've told you." Jesus pointed out that instead of anticipating the miraculous future ahead of them, they were content to settle for that which they were currently experiencing. The disciples preferred the present, and understandably so. They were human, just like you and I. As humans, we like what we have in the present. We like it because we can see it, touch it, know it. Virtually everyone is more comfortable with the known than the unknown, even if the unknown promises to be better. Here are a couple of good examples...

…a teenager more comfortable staying at home than learning how to drive
…a long-time prisoner afraid of being granted freedom
…a person surviving on fast food instead of learning to cook
…a loner uncertain about the risk of building relationships

In each of these cases, the latter is better than the former. But all require a bit of courage, and one must trust the testimonies of those that have learned to drive, tasted freedom, learned to cook, built relationships and know it's worth it.

Jesus seemed a bit startled that his disciples were more focused on worrying about his departure than they were listening to and trusting his very next words: "But in fact, it is best for you that I go away..." Jesus is saying,

Teenager – It is better that you learn to drive!
Prisoner – It is better that you are free!
Unhealthy Person – It is better that you learn to cook!
Loner – It is better that you live in community!
Disciples – It is better for you if I go away!

Hebrews 11:1, defines faith in this way: “Faith is the confidence that what we hope for will actually happen; it gives us assurance about things we cannot see.” This life with Christ – as we slowly learn – is a life of faith. It's a life of having confidence and assurance in that which we do not see. It's trusting Jesus that loving our neighbor is better for us than serving ourselves; submitting to God is better than leading our own lives; journeying through life with fellow believers is better than going at it alone; and becoming like him is better than staying like we are.

There is little doubt that Paul's words in 2 Corinthians 5:7 are difficult, “We walk by faith, not by sight (ESV).” But this is the life of the Christian. Just as a child learns to trust the good parent who knows what is best, so we trust a good God who knows what is best – both in the present and in the future.

Reflection

Today we will reflect on a simple (but not easy) question: Is there something Jesus has told you or asked of you that you have difficulty trusting him with? Are you stuck in the present, not trusting that what Jesus is doing will make for a better future?

Don't worry about solving this problem today. Instead, simply acknowledge it, and honestly tell God of your comfort with the present and your fear of the future.

If you are willing, he will move you forward soon enough. You can trust him.

Day 33

Day of Reflection

For the final two “Day of Reflection” devotionals, we will look at a classic artist’s rendering of an event in Jesus’ life on Easter weekend. The images are beautiful and touching renditions of moments in Jesus' life, and if we allow them, they can help us more deeply experience what we are reading in scripture.

We will begin with Giacomo Raffaelli’s version of the Last Supper painting. Take a few moments to concentrate on this upper room scene. Recall the event that took place there and imagine being present in that room with Jesus and the disciples.

(NOTE: If this image is too small, try an internet search for any rendition of a Last Supper painting and use the image you find to complete this reflection experience.)

Which character do you most identify with? Which character exemplifies the feelings you carry on this Sabbath day? Which did you choose, and why?

Allow yourself to remember that you are as loved by Jesus as the men were in that room, and he is just as close. Rest in that fact today, no matter which character you most identify with.

Day 34

Jesus Prays

Today let's do this a little bit different. Instead of reading the scripture now, I first want to introduce today's passage then encourage you to spend some focused time on the words of Jesus.

As we draw closer and closer to Easter, we have reached the final moments in the upper room. These are special and meaningful moments, and to me, this is one of the most beautiful and powerful passages in scripture. In John 17, we are given a rare glimpse into the specific words of Jesus' prayer life, and what we hear is important and moving.

Today's passage follows those we have already read, so in it we find Jesus sitting with his closest followers and friends. He has saved some of his most important lessons for sharing around this table, and with the most pivotal events in human history lying only a few hours ahead, Jesus speaks in prayer with God the Father. His disciples listen in, and he prays with them and for them.

Read John 17 with care, and as you do, think about and remember these things:

- The words you are reading are the very words of Christ as he talked with the Father.
- This is an intimate view of Jesus' understanding of his work and purpose and his desire for the future.
- This prayer was not only for those men in that upper room. As a disciple of Christ, Jesus' prayer is for you.

Read it slowly. Listen deeply. Keep these things in mind. And let this prayer help you better know your Savior and better grasp his love for you.

Read John 17:1-26

Reflection

Write down your first impressions and thoughts of Jesus' words. What moved you?

What were your thoughts and questions as you read verses 20-21?

Take these notes and thoughts with you throughout the day, and allow them to help you focus on the remarkable prayer of our Lord.

Day 35

Luke 22:39-45

Garden Moments

We now begin the passages that break my heart. As a friend of Jesus, and as someone (like you) who is getting to know him better and better, the scripture passages we will focus on in the coming days are difficult to read. But they are so very crucial.

I'm not naive enough to compare my suffering and pain with that of Jesus'. But this past year I had what was, for me, a Garden of Gethsemane moment. I felt God ask me to do something that would initially cause deep pain. I prayed, as Jesus did, that God would allow for another scenario; a scenario of much less pain. If there was another way, I wanted it. I prayed for it. I cried for it. But in the end, no other way was revealed, and I submitted to God's way. His will was not mine, but by his strength and because of my trust in him, I submitted.

This time as I read again Jesus' plea for an alternate way, I was struck not by what he experienced, but *how* he experienced it. I'm challenged to more intentionally follow his example the next time I have a Garden of

Gethsemane moment. Let me explain by pointing out a few of Luke's words.

"*...accompanied by the disciples...*" (v. 39)
Jesus knows he's God's son. He knows the plan is for him to die (he told his disciples this several times) and he knows the time is coming. Yet even the one and only Son of God does not travel the road alone. This fact blows my mind. I often think of Jesus as an American Superman - an individualistic immortal who takes on death all by himself. But in reality he is the fully human incarnation of God – and he does nothing alone. He has existed in the community of the Trinity for eternity, and he lived as a man in community. When he faced the greatest trial, he brought his friends to battle. The next time I go into a garden moment, I will do the same.

"*...an angel from heaven appeared and strengthened him. He prayed more fervently...*" (v, 43-44) In these words I found another way that I'm challenged to intentionally follow Christ's example. Here it is: God's help is not for our comfort (meaning ease or reduction of stress and pain). God's help is for our strength, for our ability to accomplish what he wants us to accomplish. I have to admit that when I enter Gethsemane moments, my prayer is for God to take me out of the garden, not for him to accomplish what he wants to accomplish in the garden. In different words: I pray to be delivered *from* the agony, not to be strengthened *through* the agony.

I wonder if these ways that Jesus walked through his Gethsemane moments strike you as they did me. You may be in the middle of one of those moments right now. If so, have you asked your fellow believers and friends to come with you, or are you trying to face it alone? And are you focused on asking God for an escape, or for strength?

Reflection

In your reading of this portion of Jesus' journey, were you confronted by any new perspectives or realizations? What were they?

What does it mean to you when you read of Jesus' request for an alternate way paired with his complete submission to the will of God?

If you're in one of those difficult and terrifying spots in life, I encourage you to pray without ceasing today, courageously praying for another way while also fully submitting to God's plan.

Day 36

Matthew 26:47-56, John 18:1-11

Man of His Word

We've all met people who say one thing and do another. Some do it with a disturbing amount of ease. I recently read an article about a group of people that lobbied Congress for a new bill that, if passed, will provide huge tax breaks for their industry. The problem is, this same group of men and women have repeatedly voted to raise taxes in their state. So, while they consistently support and vote for measures to raise taxes on the public at large, they are secretly petitioning congress to reduce taxes for them. Hypocritical? Seems like it. Not practicing what they preach? Definitely.

But the people we respect - the people we seek out, work with, trust, and even admire - are those that actually *do* what they say. In Matthew 21:28-32 Jesus discusses this very topic as he continues his chastisement of the religious leaders of the day. They hold everyone to one standard by what they say, but Jesus points out the hypocrisy in what they do.

When we think of Jesus' submission to the father, his complete and total giving of his life for the mission of God, we often think of yesterday's scripture passage. We quote his words from the Garden of Gethsemane: "*I want your will to be done, not mine*." But, obviously these words are only words if Jesus does nothing about them. But we see here in Matthew 26, that Jesus does just what he says. I love the way it is recorded in John 18:4. He wrote, "*Jesus fully realized all that was going to happen to him, so he stepped forward to meet them.*" Jesus told God that he would do his will, and when the time came, he stepped up to do it. We see it when he tells Judas to, "*Go ahead and do what you have come for.*(v. 50)" We see it when Peter strikes out, violently cutting off the ear of a guard, and Jesus responds with, "*Put away your sword.* (v. 52)" These are not moments of weakness and surrender in the face of a more powerful force for evil. Rather, these are moments of strength when Jesus is giving in to a more powerful force for good. Jesus is fully submitting to his father, just as he said he would.

This is the holy example of our Jesus. He really is going with God's will over his own. He really is going to give his life as a ransom for many. He really is a man of his word.

Reflection

Does it require more strength to fight or to submit?

How do you see the power of Jesus' word at play in this scene?

Jesus is completely willing to do the Father's work. As you go about your day, focus on the word "willing" and specifically pray for God's strength to willingly do what he asks you to do.

Day 37

Mark 14:53-65

Caiaphas, Did You Know?

There is a sad and terrible irony to Jesus' appearance before Caiaphas. Caiaphas, as high priest of Israel, was an ancestor of Aaron, the first great priest of the people of God. The high priest's role was to serve as the intermediary between God and the people of Israel, and only he could offer sacrifices to God for the sins of the people.

There's a Christmas song called, "Mary, Did You Know?" Have you heard it? It is a beautiful and haunting song that wonders at the experience of Mary, the mother of God. The song asks, "Mary did you know this child that you delivered would soon deliver you?" and did you know "When you kiss your little baby, you kiss the face of God?" I wonder similar questions for Caiaphas.

Caiaphas, did you know that when Jesus entered your home, your home became the Holy of Holies?

Caiaphas, as high priest who has stood in the presence of God, did you recognize him when you were standing with Jesus?

Caiaphas, did you know thc one you led to slaughter was God's sacrifice for you?

The writer of Hebrews describes the sacrificial system of first-century Judaism as "only a copy, a shadow of the real one in heaven.(v. 8:5)" I can't help but wonder if Caiaphas had any idea that he would be the last to bare the shadow of a sacrificial system made obsolete by the Lamb of God. Caiaphas, did you know? There stood the true and better high priest, the one who would serve as the sacrifice for Caiaphas' sin, your sin, my sin, and the sins of the world. There stood the high priest who was, and always will be, thc only mediator between God and man.

In Mark 14, the high priest of Jerusalem met the High Priest of Heaven and he denied him, accused him, and planned his execution. Each day we have the same choice. As lord of our own lives, we come face to face with the Lord of all life, and we have the opportunity to deny, accuse, and execute the presence of God in our lives. It sounds harsh, but like Caiaphas, we must ask "Are you the Messiah?" and when he answers, "I AM," we can choose our way or his. One leads to death. One leads to life.

Reflection

Recall a time when you looked into the face of God and refused to acknowledge him as Lord of your life. What was that like?

What is it like now? When Jesus, like with Caiaphas, meets you where you are, how do you respond?

Day 38

Luke 22:54-64

Denial

In 2004, a movie about the last hours of Jesus' life set box office records. It was called, "The Passion of the Christ." You may have seen it. It's a gruesomely accurate portrayal of the kind of beating and torture that prisoners experienced at the hands of Roman centurions on their way to execution by Roman cross. It's the kind of death Jesus experienced. I rarely talk with a follower of Christ who was not moved by the film. Many have cried, others refuse to watch it. Of those who refuse, their reasoning is not the blood and gore by itself, but specifically it's the bloody and gory portrayal of their Lord's death. It's difficult to watch. It brings tears.

I've seen it a handful of times, always around this time of year, and I also find myself with tear-laden eyes at one point in the movie. But it is not because of the injustice, the beating, and the brutal death of my Savior. My tears flow at a different point in the movie. My tears flow at Peter's denial.

The movie recreates the scene from today's passage

just as it is described in scripture. It's the dark of night, and as Jesus is being tried Peter seems to be faithfully following his Rabbi at a safe distance. He can't follow too closely because the religious elite are out for blood, and they have formed an angry mob that will have little to no discretion regarding who they beat or kill. So, Peter stands back but remains deeply concerned. When reading the story, I'm certain he's waiting for the right moment to help. I'm hopeful, convinced that soon he will jump in and defend his friend. Right?

But then, the first servant girl stares at him and points him out. A second agrees. A third hears his Galilean accent and joins in their claims that he's a follower of Christ. Before he can stop himself, Peter does what he swore he would never do. He denies any association with Jesus at all. The rooster crows, and as the actor playing Peter runs from the scene, I begin to cry.

I cry at this scene because it is too often a retelling not only of Peter's story, but of my story. When the going gets tough - when the surrounding crowd seems to be carried away in an anti-Jesus sentiment - I follow at a distance. I keep warm by the fire with the unconcerned, contemplating the perfect moment for me to jump to Jesus' defense, protect the reputation of my fellow Christians, or aid the needy and broken.

And before I summon the courage to act, someone calls me out. My actions, if not always my words, profess my denial of Jesus. And sometimes, like during the movie, I cry.

But the beauty of Peter's story, and of mine, is that God does not leave us there in our denial and fear. He could. He's God. He doesn't need our assistance. But because he is ferociously in love with us, and because he so longs to be in relationship with us, he runs after us and restores us by his grace. I, like Peter, am a glad and thankful recipient of such overwhelming mercy. And I hope, also like Peter, that my denial of him now will remind me of his devotion to me later, and I will more bravely and faithfully face those who would accuse my Jesus. I hope.

Reflection

How does Peter’s denial affect you? When was the last time you stood back and warmed yourself by the fire while Jesus (or another innocent) was wrongly accused?

What is your honest response to these thoughts?

Want to join me in doing something else difficult? Spend a few moments today and ask God to reveal the areas, situations, or relationships where you deny being a follower of his. Recognize his loving and accurate conviction, and spend some time talking with him about it and praying for strength to obey.

Day 39

John 18:19-40

Still Changing

In first-century Jerusalem, there was no such thing as separation of church and state. The king and magistrates, as well as the high priests, carried great authority, and each could try someone based on violation of laws against the state or laws against the temple. So when Jesus' first trial at the high priest's house concluded, the mob transported Jesus to Pilate to endure a second one. Why worry with two trials? The leading priests were so threatened by Jesus, and so unwilling to entertain that the Kingdom of God was different than they imagined, that their goal was death. Even with all their power, the priests in Jewish court could not render the death penalty. But the magistrates in a Roman one could.

I'll continue with the same kind of questioning I applied to Caiaphas a few days ago: did Pilate, a governor under King Caesar, realize he was talking with the King of Kings? Did he realize he was standing face-to-face with the one who would return from heaven in the last days to claim his rightful place as the one good ruler of all creation? No. No he didn't.

And I think we forget too.

There's a strange sense of ambivalence with Pilate. Except for a mysterious message delivered in a dream to his wife (Matthew 27:19), there is nothing about this Jesus that strikes Pilate as criminal or dangerous. He's simply another "heretic" that needs to be controlled by the priests in their court of law. And he does his best to dismiss Jesus.

And I think we do the same thing.

Most of you reading this are Christian. You have taken notice of Jesus, and he is more than a dismissible religious guru. Something about him and his story has been meaningful to you. Most likely it has changed you. But is it *still* changing you? Are your interactions with Jesus still shaping and changing your life? Do you love people more today than you did yesterday? Are you more aware of those who are poor, heartbroken, and in trouble? Do you continue to understand the depth of your own sin, and does it continually lead you to repentance? Does evil in the world lead you to cry out for Jesus more and more?

You and I have celebrated many a Christmas and Easter, but we can subtly be fooled into believing, like

Pilate, that this is just another day and Jesus doesn't change it. Easter is coming. Jesus is here. And he's a life changer. But we must not dismiss him.

Reflection

Today, reminisce about the first time you met Jesus (whether 20 years ago or 20 days ago). What impact did he have and did he change your life? If so, in what ways? If not, why not?

In what ways is Jesus still changing your life?

If you have dismissed Jesus, prayerfully commit to engage him today, and allow him the freedom to change your life. The changes will only be for the better.

Day 40

Day of Reflection

Below is Gustave Dore's depiction of Pontius Pilate presenting a scourged Christ to the angry mob. Just like last week, take a few reflective moments to observe this scene: the setting, the people, the expressions, their gestures, and their emotions.

As you take time to reflect on the artist's recreation of the final events we've been reading from scripture this week, which characters stand out to you? Which do you identify with?

Now draw a picture of your own in your mind. Use your imagination to think about what lies ahead for Jesus. Prepare yourself for this coming week as we will read and reflect on Jesus' final moments before the grave and his first moments after it.

Day 41

John 19:1-16

Control

Pilate sees in Jesus what he has seen in no other man he's faced, including Caesar. He sees real power, real control. In today's scripture, Pilate is on the brink of losing control. The angry mob is trying to force his hand, and when they cry out accusing him of being "no friend to Caesar," he caves into their villainous demands. He's fighting hard to regain control, squelch an uprising, and assure himself a long career by avoiding any appearance of defying Caesar.

And in the middle of all the chaos, Jesus offers Pilate a startling amount of clarity. Read verses 7-11 again. Do you see it? Do you see who has control? Do you see who really wields the power here? It's not where you would expect it, and it went virtually unseen by every member of the religious leadership, every Roman centurion, and every member of the blood-thirsty mob. But Pilate sees it face to face. Jesus is not being overpowered by a fearful Jewish mob or Roman authorities. Jesus is overpowering death so we can live fearless lives.

As this week unfolds - as we march towards Good Friday and the execution that changed the world forever - don't forget who is in control.

There is a heretical theology of the crucifixion that is sometimes referred to as "divine child abuse." The theory is this; a wrathful God unjustly kills his innocent son to somehow pay the debt for our sin. Does that sound right? Parts of it should. That's the problem with heresy. It's *almost* true. Or as my former pastor defined it, "Heresy is truth out of balance." The problem with that view of the crucifixion is three-fold: it dismisses the Trinity, it neglects the cost of sin, and it misconstrues God's love. Christ did not go to the cross *so* God could love us. Christ went to the cross *because* God already does (John 3:16, John 15:12-13, John 10:17-18, 1 John 4:9-10).

In the middle of your own chaos, do not forget this: sin and death did not conquer an unwilling Jesus, but rather a willing Jesus conquered sin and death. In those moments, Pilate knew it. And in these moments, we need to know it.

"*You would have no power over me at all unless it were given to you from above.*"

This is the knowledge Jesus holds in the face of death,

and these are the words Jesus gives to an ego-centric Pilate. As the final minutes pass and the cross draws nearer, your God was never more in control.

Reflection

What are the "angry mobs" and Pontius Pilates in your life? What are the circumstances, people, or problems that seem to have more power than God? Take a moment to recognize and name them.

Read verse 11 again, but instead of Pilate as the recipient of these words, let God point them instead to the obstacle you named above, and allow yourself to rest in the fact that nothing is out of God's sight and control.

Day 42

Matthew 27:27-44

Everyone Needs a King

A few years ago I heard a sermon by Dr. Timothy Keller in which he made some intriguing and insightful comments about kings. His first comment was, “Everyone wants a king.” Everyone wants and needs someone, or something, to be the ultimate authority in their lives, and if that ultimate authority is not God, then every individual and every culture will choose an inferior replacement. It has happened throughout all of history. Kings (or their equivalent) have been the standard for political leadership for the majority of world history. Israel clamored for a king in 1 Samuel 8 instead of keeping God as their sole authority. Even in our modern, king-less culture, we crown de facto kings, thrusting celebrities and sports heroes into the role of authority by our near deification of them. They may not lead us politically, but we mimic their opinions, lifestyles, and choices.

We will all deify something or someone because, as Dr. Keller says, “We all need a king.”

The soldiers in Caesar’s army can’t seem to help but

make fun of this lowly Jesus who claimed to be “King of the Jews.” After all, they knew who was king of the Jews - it was Caesar - and they had watched him grow to power and had thrived, in many ways, under his leadership. So who wouldn’t mock a powerless man claiming to be king? They did and others joined in as they murdered this imposter.

As you observe the people around you, you'll see the same. Watch closely and you'll see people who have made something or someone king in their life, and once this person or thing is given authority there is no room for a king like Jesus. So they mock him. They beat him down with their words and their denial in hopes that he will just die.

But something lacks in the service of a king who is not really the King. Think about it.

Don't we grow tired of kings that offer no lasting peace? Don't we tire of kings that hold out an ideal that always makes us a failure? And aren't we wearied by kings we must chase but who never chase us?

Don’t you wish your king understood what it was like to live a life like yours? Don’t you wish there was a king who had greater authority than the Pilates in your life?

There is one such king. And he is the only real king. He is King Jesus.

And it's true – King Jesus doesn't look like the kings we know and the kings we crown. But that is because he isn't like those kings.

Jesus offers peace (Phil 4:6-7).
In Christ you are not a failure (Rom 8:1-3).
God pursued you first (John 15:16, Eph 1:4-5).
Jesus experienced the human condition (Heb 2:18, 4:15).
There is none with greater authority than God (Matt 28:18, Eph 1:21-22).

The soldiers didn't recognize him. Our lost friends and family don't recognize him. Many Christians at many points in life don't recognize him. But, he is no less the king.

Reflection

Is Jesus the one real king of your life?

Spend the day reflecting on the answer to that question. If he is not, ask yourself honestly, "How peace-giving, satisfying, understanding, and loving are the other kings in my life?"

Day 43

Luke 23:26-43, John 19:17-27

God Revealed

Jesus Christ is God. He is the incarnation, or the assumption of human form and nature of a loving, forgiving, selfless, and powerful God who reigns in heaven and desires all men to share eternity with him. These truths can be found in all of scripture, in the lives of his followers, and in particular here: in Jesus on the cross. I don't mean symbolically. I mean literally.

"Adversity does not build character, it reveals it." There's some real truth to this quote by James Lane Allen, an American novelist. If you want to see what people are really like, watch them when life is difficult, when they are in pain, or when they are facing death. During the first century there was no greater physical adversity than Roman crucifixion. The role of Roman executioners was not to simply kill you; their role was to make dying a long and excruciatingly painful experience. Their goal was to make you wish you were dead already.

I don't write this to hyperbolize. I write this to help

you understand a pain that very few people have experienced. It was the kind of adversity that rather than reveal your character, would create a new one. Torture will make the most loving and selfless person hate his enemy and experience and spew vitriol as deep and caustic as the pain. This is why the cross does not only lead to the death necessary to save us, but reveals to us the heart of the God who saves us.

"Father, forgive them."

"I assure you, today you will be with me in paradise."

"Dear woman, here is your son."

God does not only preach forgiveness, he gives it. God does not only desire for all men to have eternal life, he grants it. God does not only command us to think of others first, he does it.

Hanging from a tree by his own bones, his skin and muscle ripped off his back, and thorns piercing his temples, the character of God is truly uncovered. And the criminal next to him, who becomes the first beneficiary of the new covenant, recognizes and speaks the even more miraculous truth of this painfully revealing event: "*We deserve to die for our crimes, but this man hasn't done anything wrong.*"

Have you ever known a love like this? It is *your* sin that leads to death. It is *my* body that deserves ruthless pain and torture. It is *your* disobedience that flagrantly mocks the Holy God. It is *my* sinfulness that causes others pain and leads them astray. And yet it was HE - innocent Jesus - who was spit on, stripped, beaten, whipped, and hammered by stake to the splintered wood of a hastily cut tree. JESUS. Not you. Not me.

That is the revealed character of God. That is the God you serve. That is the God who has saved you and loved you.

Reflection

Read 1 Peter 2:24....***"He*** *himself* ***bore our sins*** *in his body on the tree, so that we might die to sins and live for righteousness;* ***by his wounds you have been healed."***

What does this verse say about our salvation (emphases added by me)? Who is responsible?

Spend some time expressing your gratitude to him - in prayer, song, art, written words - or any way you like.

Day 44

Luke 23:44-49, John 19:28-42

Death

Think back to the beginning of Jesus' life and imagine the scene at his Christmas time arrival. I know we are drawing close to Easter, so this may be cause for some Christian holiday confusion, but bear with me. Picture Jesus in the manger. Now Mary and Joseph. Can you see them? Now imagine their visitors. Among them were the three wise men. What did they bring? Yes - Gold, Frankincense, and Myrrh.

A few Advent seasons ago, my pastor pointed out the significance of these gifts in a way I had never thought of before. Each gift is a meaningful symbol. The first is gold – the substance of kings. A gift fit for the King of Kings. Second is frankincense – incense burned as a holy aroma by the Priest. A gift fit for the true high priest. That leaves myrrh. Do you know what myrrh was? Myrrh was a traditional ointment for burial. It was an embalming fluid. It was the same myrrh that Joseph of Arimathea and Nicodemus used thirty-three years later to bury the dead Jesus. Isn't it a bit offensive to bring the scent of death to the celebration of new life? Myrrh is kind of a strange gift for a child.

But, Jesus was not simply any child, and as peculiar as it must have seemed, the myrrh was as fitting a symbol as the gold and frankincense. Yes, this child of God was king and high priest, but he was also the great sacrifice. He would live for a purpose and he would die for a purpose. This was the plan from the beginning.

God does not defeat death by executive order. He doesn't make a call from a distant place for someone else to take care of the hard work for him. He does it himself.

There's a phrase you may have heard: "You can't win a game you don't play." It's true. It would be strange to claim victory at chess without ever sitting down at a board and moving a pawn. A high school athlete does not receive a trophy for a sport she's never taken the field in. To win something, you must play it. To defeat something, you must battle it. To destroy something, you must face it.

This is why Jesus' death is absolutely necessary. Our sin brings death into the world making it the end of all our lives and separating us from God. Our rebellion has brought on consequences that we cannot remedy on our own, and without any sort of intervention this is how it would have stayed. But in his mercy, the God who created us volunteered to enter the game, face the enemy, taste the consequence of our rebellion, and destroy it forever. So he died. Real death. His friends brought the myrrh for embalming and they laid his cold, lifeless body in a tomb.

Only then was he able to win. Only with a Good Friday do we get an Easter Sunday.

Reflection

In our feel good society, it's not politically correct to talk about death. But today, I want you to think about it. You may be afraid of it, you may be ambivalent to it, or you may simply never think about it. But it is the reality of your sin. And only Jesus has conquered it – forever.

If you are a follower of Christ, spend the day thanking Jesus for defeating our greatest enemy. If you are not – or if you are uncertain – take seriously the truth of death. And remember that it is only conquered through the work, power, and grace of Jesus Christ.

Day 45

The Dark Before the Dawn

Through this Lent devotional, we have read the Gospel accounts of Jesus' road to the cross and have relived his teaching, betrayal, crucifixion, and his death. Today, as you continue to contemplate all that his death has meant, read the following verses and passages in lieu of a written devotion.

Enjoy all of them, a few of them, or choose just one to meditate on throughout the day. As you read and pray, allow God's word to lead you into worship and gratitude for the completion of God's unbelievable work. Make this a silent day of reflection as you remember all that God has accomplished.

Isaiah 53:2-12

Mark 10:45

John 10:11

John 10:17-18

John 12:20-28

John 15:13

Romans 5:8

Romans 8:3

2 Corinthians 5:21

Colossians 1:15-20

Hebrews 7:26-28

Reflection

Take time to record in writing your thoughts, feelings, and prayers as you think about what this weekend signifies and celebrates.

Day 46

John 20:1-31

Life

There is no doubt that the morning was dark. The hour held an absence of light and a vacancy of joy as Mary and the women visited the tomb. All that filled their weary minds were the painful unwanted memories of the last 72 hours, and the optimism that characterized their lives with Jesus was gone. Then suddenly, as if someone struck a match in the pitch black, an unexpected sight caused their hearts to race. Jesus' body was gone. Their thoughts of the past were instantly wiped away and all their senses, thoughts, and emotions were intensely focused on the present moment and the only important question: where is he?

Amid the confusion, faint traces of Jesus' mysterious words from the past crept back into the present: he would be killed but on the third day he would be raised from the dead. As their minds sought to connect the dots, the page on a dark chapter began to close and the hope of a blank page began to open. Like the moments before your bride walks down the aisle, or the night before you go into labor, there's a sense that soon - very soon - everything is going to change.

And then it did.

"*'Mary!' Jesus said. She turned to him and cried out, 'Raboni!'*"(v. 16) Later his disciples were gathered in fear and "*Suddenly, Jesus was standing there among them*!" (v. 19) In the middle of their grief, the one they were mourning appeared back from the dead!

Unbelievable, right!? Can you imagine that?

Believe it or not, I have a friend who can. His dad was pronounced dead, and several minutes later, he was resuscitated. He's alive today to share the incredible story. The friends of Jesus saw some miraculous things too. Lazarus was dead. A young girl was dead. But so was my friend's dad and a bunch of other people who have "walked towards the light" and lived tell about it. But there is one crucial difference: None of these people raised themselves. Not one. And eventually, all of them will die. Just like the rest of us.

When Jesus walked out of the tomb, he did it of his own accord. He did it because he is God and he alone could conquer death forever. In that one act of holy power he reversed the curse of our many acts of unholy rebellion. Jesus lived the sinless life none of us will, he willingly died the death all of us deserve, and he powerfully rose again so all of us can.

"He lives, He lives! Christ Jesus lives today! He walks with me and talks with me along life's narrow way" wrote Alfred H. Ackley, the great hymn writer. There is nothing in the world worth celebrating more than the one who has conquered death forever and who offers us life like we could never know without him. This is what we celebrate on Easter Sunday and each day we walk with him.

He is alive! Turn up the music, enjoy the food, hug and love your family, friends, and neighbors, for today has changed everything. "*Jesus is the Messiah, the Son of God, and by believing in him you will have life by the power of his name.*" (v. 31)

Reflection

Imagine you were there; a disciple who loved and followed Jesus and witnessed his resurrection. Picture the day and imagine the feelings. How would you have celebrated? Spend a few minutes imagining that party and how the joy with which you would live life afterwards.

Now imagine you are here; a disciple who loves and follows Jesus who can bear witness to his resurrection through the authority of scripture and the Holy Spirit in your life. What kind of party does that make you want to throw and what kind of joy does that give you today?

That's life. *That's* the Kingdom of God. Now go live in it.

Day 47

Day of Reflection

He is Risen! He is Risen Indeed! Hallelujah!

"*This is the day the Lord has made. We will rejoice and be glad in it!*" writes the Psalmist who knew God.

And Paul, who met the risen Christ, follows it with these powerful words from Romans 8:31-39.

Let your heart sing these verses as you celebrate today and share this life-giving good news with everyone you know.

> "***What shall we say about such wonderful things as these? If God is for us, who can ever be against us? Since he did not spare even his own Son but gave him up for us all, won't he also give us everything else? Who dares accuse us whom God has chosen as his own? No one—for God himself has given us right standing with himself. Who then will condemn us? No one—for Christ Jesus died for us and was raised to life for us,***

and he is sitting in the place of honor at God's right hand, pleading for us. Can anything ever separate us from Christ's love? Does it mean he no longer loves us if we have trouble or calamity, or are persecuted, or hungry, or destitute, or in danger, or threatened with death? (As the scriptures say, "For your sake we are killed every day; we are being slaughtered like sheep.") No, despite all these things, overwhelming victory is ours through Christ, who loved us. And I am convinced that nothing can ever separate us from God's love. Neither death nor life, neither angels nor demons, neither our fears for today nor our worries about tomorrow—not even the powers of hell can separate us from God's love. No power in the sky above or in the earth below—indeed, nothing in all creation will ever be able to separate us from the love of God that is revealed in Christ Jesus our Lord."

Amen and Amen.

Reflection

Read Paul's words again and decide now how Jesus' victory over death will inspire and shape your words and actions in the coming days, weeks, months, and years.

He is risen! He is risen, indeed.

The Next 47 Days....

If you used this Bible study and devotion as preparation for celebrating Easter, or if simply as a forty-seven day walk through Jesus' final earthly days, I hope you won't stop here. Instead, I encourage you to commit to walking through the next forty-seven days in celebration of Christ's resurrection. Similar to the way you used the past six weeks to prepare daily for Jesus' death, use the next six weeks to celebrate his defeat of death. I hope you will continue to read, pray, and reflect daily in celebration of the victory he has won.

God is good, and in his son Jesus Christ, there is much to celebrate and much to share with the world around us.

If you have any thoughts or personal reflections on what you have read, or if you would like to share how God moved, touched, or changed you during these forty-seven days, please contact me at ChristopherGreerWriter@gmail.com I would love to hear from you!

You can also find my Christmas devotional, *Christmas*

Is Coming, at Amazon.com. *Christmas Is Coming,* is a thoughtful follow-up to *Easter Is Coming* and will help you prepare for and celebrate Christmas in a powerful way.

About the Author:

Christopher Greer is a writer, speaker, and church leader. He lives with his wife in Southern California. You can read more of his writing at www.Christopher-Greer.com and www.Trochia.org.

NOTES

NOTES

NOTES

45790253R00088

Made in the USA
San Bernardino, CA
17 February 2017